ONE FOR THE
MEMORY BANKS

ONE FOR THE
MEMORY BANKS

LUKE REESE

EDITED BY
MADELINE REESE

Nº 9
PUBLISHING
HOUSE

No. 9 Publishing House in cooperation with Blue Raspberry Productions.

Illustrations by Enid Day.
Design & layout by Bancroft Graphics.

All inquiries should be addressed to: No. 9 Publishing House
Email: info@no9publishinghouse.com

Printed in Canada

10 9 8 7 6 5 4 3 2 1

ISBN 978-1-7351218-0-2

To Allan Bond and Angus Moir

Contents

Author's Note

~

The following are all real events that took place with real people.

These are my memories. They are inexact. I have kept scorecards, notes, signed balls, bottles, hats, clubs, etc. I took notes on many of these events shortly after they happened. I have consulted with all the people who were present in each case to reconstruct dialogue. Precisely re-creating dialogue among two or more Irishmen is a virtual impossibility—too many words, too fast. All parties present agree that the gist is correct. Post-round alcohol was usually involved. I take full responsibility for any factual errors.

CHAPTER I

~

RUB OF THE GREEN

Number fifteen played downwind that day, crossing back to the linksland near the sea. We had both made a lot of pars and a few bogeys—much better than I normally played. Single-digit Bondy had been there a million times, but I was light years out of my comfort zone. I could feel the pressure. We were in a tight match. Bondy hit his drive down the middle. Throat dry, my head spun. I might actually beat him. My swing shortened dramatically on the tee shot. Through a wry grin, a Scottish voice mumbled, "A wee bit quick on that one, young Mr. Reese. Not your finest." Into the right rough it flew. It might be in deep. Won't know till I get up there. Please, don't be lost.

Please...don't be lost...

MY OPPONENT

Imagine a 50-something-year-old Scotsman. Perhaps you see a kilt-wearing Sean Connery standing on the ramparts of his battle-worn castle overlooking the barren highlands. Or James Bond bedecked in a tuxedo at a casino, daringly out-thinking his foes and romancing all women who cross his path. Those are the myths.

Reality offered a different Bond. Allan Bond, age 52. Called Bondy by all who knew him. My fierce and witty opponent. This large-boned man projected height and strength, with silvery hair worn slightly over the ears. His dress was always appropriate, but never dashing. There was little risk of hearing your wife mutter under her breath, "I wish you'd dress more like Allan Bond."

Determined, his eyes could fix a menacing look but frequently with a twinkle. What he said, he meant. I was glad that we met in 1994, rather than as opposing warriors during an *Outlander* or *Braveheart* time warp. He and I fought on more modern battlefields—those with eighteen holes. Though I was his boss at work, Bondy always seemed to get the better of me on the golf course...a fact he never let me forget.

Though Scottish clan life had abated over the centuries, respect for authority had been firmly ingrained in Bondy, but he couldn't resist flashing a knowing grin. Growing up on the west coast of Scotland in the '50s, he caddied for high-handicap, upper-class gentlemen, who were quick to dress down a young wispy lad for causing their wayward putts. In his words, "I'll tell ya this...I knew who the boss was...held the flag stick and kept my mouth shut. Didn't get paid much. Didn't get fired. Learnt a lot about life caddying for bad golfers."

He idolized his grandfather who captained a munitions ship in World War II, avoiding mines and U-boats. Allan was a serious pupil in the excellent Scottish school system whose studies included French and Latin. His love of geography whetted his appetite to see the world. Further, he wanted to emulate his grandfather and have his own ship to command. At age fifteen, over the objections of his parents, he joined the Merchant Navy. After nearly five exciting and rewarding years at sea, he failed his eye exam. Sadly, the now worldly Bondy had to immediately come home. Dreams dashed. Needed to find a job.

In 1962, while Arnold Palmer won The Open at Royal Troon, Sam Snead cut a ceremonial ribbon opening the Wilson Sporting Goods golf club factory a few miles down the road in Bondy's hometown of Irvine. Dark and spartan, the Wilson factory building could have been confused for a local penitentiary. But, as Bondy said, "A new factory making golf clubs was better than working at a paper mill." Fittingly, Bondy walked in and asked for work. As he would joke, "Somebody must have had too much to drink the night before and not shown up. They begrudgingly let me repair golf clubs. No idea what that meant...

but they said they were going to pay me. Showed up the next day...ne'er left."

Hardworking and whip-smart, Bondy did not intend to repair clubs in the back of the factory for long. His bosses noticed him, and he was given a sales rep job. Multiple promotions later, he became Wilson's beloved UK sales manager. "Would have gotten fired repairing clubs," he would laugh. "Couldn't get the heads on straight. Probably a few golfers hook or slice because of me."

Wilson hired me at age 33 in the early fall of 1994, as the export manager in charge of some small markets that sold both tennis and golf. That is when I met veteran UK sales manager, Bondy.

At the end of a day of meetings at our offices in Germany, Bondy put his bear paw on my shoulder. "Young lad, I've watched you in meetings all day. You could sell life insurance to dead people...and you know yer tennis... but learn golf. Big growth there." Great advice. Doubt he knew my name. He went back to the UK, and I stayed in Germany none the wiser.

As a solid, former college tennis player, I understood tennis. In contrast, golf was a blank slate. I followed Bondy's direct advice and decided to learn. I had hit millions of tennis balls...

What could be hard about golf? A stick. A ball. Not even moving.

After a quick lesson from a low handicapper, I worked on a short takeaway and follow-through. At work, my office was near the Wilson warehouse on the ground floor. I loved being near the action (and the wide hallways). Before and after work hours, I would hit Wiffle golf balls in the hallway to develop my swing. I left a lot of marks on the industrial carpet, and the balls sometimes even made it 50 feet to the warehouse door.

With a few months of practice under my belt, I thought it time to ask Bondy to critique my swing. His answer came in a Scottish brogue with enormous authority, intended for all within earshot: "As a golfer, you'd make a fine salesman."

I provided all the fuel he needed to stoke his fire when I asked, "What would you fix?" Several others heard me and leaned in. In the tradition of Winston Churchill, he was at his best in front of a crowd, and to Bondy's delight, he now had an audience: "I'm certainly not a golf instructor myself...but follow my simple rule when standing in front of a golf account...never..."

He brought the small crowd in further. By now, everyone had put down their coffee cups and leaned in.

"And I mean never...touch a club as if you are going to swing it. Don't waggle—don't address the ball. Hold the club close to the head and hand it to the pro. You tell them why the club is so good and how much it costs. Then you can hold a pen and paper and write orders."

Delighted chuckles from the crowd.

Though the brunt of the joke, I immediately sensed what all the others knew about Bondy. He was the center of a great party. The next week a package arrived at my office in Munich postmarked from London. It was from Bondy. He had sent me a copy of Donald Steel's *Classic Golf Links* with a note: *"Mr. Reese, work on your swing. We'll play some of these places. Start at page 30. This is real golf. Bondy."* We immediately became friends, despite our 17-year age difference.

In 1995, I became the sales manager for Europe and then the president of the division the following year. We had a lot to do. Over the previous several years, Wilson had tragically followed a low-end, fast-moving consumer goods strategy. I wanted to follow Titleist's strategy—and do it for the long term. If they could make the best technical products and have the best relationships with their accounts, why couldn't we? At Wilson, we did this in tennis. But in golf, years of short-term distribution decisions had robbed us of our former glory. They had changed directions like a kite in a tornado—chasing quarter-end targets.

The UK market was crucial for golf, and I needed to hire a new managing director for the UK to help me implement these changes.

All the candidates seemed to be cut from the same cloth. Articulate. Well-educated. Charming. Impeccably dressed. In one interview, a candidate remarked, "One of my challenges would be to learn everything Allan Bond knows before he retires."

It had not occurred to him that Bondy might be his competitor. Previous senior management had always gone for flashy MBA types, creating a revolving door of well-meaning, but generally ineffective, hires. By the time Bondy's bosses figured out which end of the stick you used to hit the ball, they were gone. Bondy was relegated to the corporate version of the Land of Forgotten Toys.

I didn't say a word, just listened, as the candidate built the case for Bondy. He fit the bill perfectly. But the only way this long-term strategy could work was if Bondy made it his own.

After the meeting, I asked Bondy to come in for an interview. Bondy and I spent hours discussing the new direction. We were in agreement.

When I flew to London to offer Bondy the job, he was visibly moved: "I'm on your team, boss. If there are any problems, we'll be in a foxhole together...guns pointing out. You'll never hear anything out of me except technical, premium racquets and clubs...and every account will be treated like Augusta."

Bondy's word was all I needed.

We shook hands and started to leave for lunch. Then he smiled, "Oh, and one more thing, before I accept...don't think this means I'll be giving you extra strokes. You're starting to actually hit the ball...but you still can't putt." Then he laughed so hard he started coughing.

A few weeks later, the candidate who had laid out the case for Bondy called me and said, "As soon as I said that about Bondy, it struck me that you would hire him. He's your kind of guy. Great leader and funny as hell."

Bondy told me years later, "I truly thought you were only interviewing me out of courtesy." He had no idea how excited I was to have him. The man hated to spend money and led his team like a combination drill sergeant and comedian. They would follow him up any hill. Justifying my faith in him, Bondy rallied his troops behind a new high margin, superstar product strategy and completely modified the UK sales and marketing efforts. He and his team wound up crushing their sales and profit numbers for several years in a row in both tennis and golf.

THE MATCH

In the fall of '96, Bondy asked me to speak at the UK sales meeting in Scotland.

After the meeting, Bondy asked, "Exactly what time is your flight back to London?" I looked at my watch: we had several hours to kill. The drive to Edinburgh would lead past several links courses.

"Our work is done," he said. "Let's push our flights back and get in a quick match. It's rumored that there are a few somewhat passable tracks in these parts. Can we find one in that *Classic Golf Links* book I gave you?" I didn't need to open the book to tell him which ones were on the direct path to the airport. I had memorized it. Waving a new links course in front of me inspired quick action.

As long as we played in less than three hours, we'd be fine. We changed plane tickets and got an open tee time just down the road at Lundin Golf Club. On a mission, Bondy and I raced into the town of Lundin Links. Two business partners and good friends, grinning ear to ear, whisked away in a tiny, gear-stuffed rental car. We were about to steal eighteen extra holes from life.

LUNDIN LINKS

Like so many Scottish clubs, Lundin is a classic links course with an intriguing history. In the late 1800s, the course was an out-and-back links course right along the Firth of Forth, shared by multiple golfing societies from the neighboring towns of Lundin Links and Leven.

The Lundin club members were a bit stuffier than those from Leven. Not a great mix.

In 1909, they decided to go their separate ways. Without bloodshed, but with lots of rancor, the two towns split their course, with each club taking nine holes. They built a stone wall between what became the new fifth holes of each course.

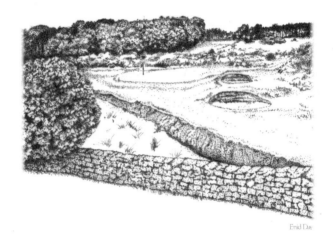

Enid Day

Each club had to add another nine holes on less linksy property farther inland. As to the links holes near the sea, they had hard and firm sand-based fairways and greens. There were no trees. Bunkers were round and deep. They had rumpled natural fairways. A stiff breeze blew in the salty smell of the sea. The sea almost faded seamlessly into the multihued grey sky.

As beautiful as links courses are, many come with a view of smokestacks in the distance. Somehow, they fit in. Sort of like cigarette smoke in a Parisian café. It belongs.

Match Play

Golf in the UK is almost exclusively centered on match play. In match play, there are essentially eighteen individual battles. The score is kept in relationship to the opponent. Win the first hole and you are one up. Lose the first hole and you are one down. If you are five holes ahead with only four holes left to play, you have just won five and four.

In my many years playing golf in the UK, I don't think I have ever heard a player, other than a stray American, say, "I shot an 81" or "I shot a 92." The answer to "How did you play?" is "Played pretty well. We won two and one."

Most of all, they play fast—less than three hours for a group of four.

Within a year and a half of starting, I could manage a score in the low 90s, but my putting was atrocious. Every time I stood over a long putt, I wondered if I would still have ten feet for the second. And when I stood over a short putt, I would think about how bummed I would be when I missed it. A round would include maybe six or seven greens in regulation and a bunch of good chips and bunker shots. But two-putting was as elusive as lasting peace in the Middle East.

After our first few rounds together, Bondy coached, "Young Mr. Reese, take a wider stance to balance against the wind. Don't squeeze the life out of the putter. Don't look up too early. If you hear the ball make a pleasant sound as it finds its home underground, you'll know you've done all right." He then smirked. "If you don't hear a sound, it will be me smiling."

Thanks to his putting advice, I was playing to a thirteen. Age had moved Bondy from low single-digit to an eight. He gave me three-quarters of the difference in our handicaps, which is typical for match play in the UK. Four strokes.

Let the games begin.

Donning turtlenecks, sweaters, and terrible windbreakers, we stopped by the pro shop, paid the modest green fee, and hurried to the first tee.

As a golf companion, Bondy ranked in my top five. As a golf partner, he was in my top two. As an opponent, he was number one. He was never out of a hole and never gave up. Over the years, I've seen him sink far too many putts after striping a five wood from 190 yards. He would then say, "Simple up and down, eh, Mr. Reese?" If anything brought Bondy greater pleasure than beating me,

I was not aware of it. I suspect a few others would say the same.

At Lundin, the first hole played into a two-club wind—approximately twenty mph. This was just a wee breeze in Scotland. Holes one and eighteen share a wide-open fairway. Lundin, as is typical of many links courses, has few practice facilities to speak of, so the drive on the first hole is frequently an easy place to stretch the back. After a couple of stiff practice swings, Bondy ambled to the tee box and put his tee in the ground. He looked back at me: "Here's one for the memory banks. Likely an easy victory for old Bondy then a nice nap on the plane ride home."

He then hit a nasty, low squirmer that tailed right. Not to be outdone, I took a hard swing. The ball popped up in the air. Great start.

We played the first four holes briskly, into the fresh breeze. The smell of the sea invigorated us.

The fifth hole is a beautiful downhill short par-three. The stone wall running the length of the hole evokes images of Scots dividing a great course. My opponent personified centuries of stubbornness. True to form, Bondy refused to make bogey. After mishitting his tee shot, he chipped to seven feet. Then with his wide stance and Arnold Palmer putting style—feet wide but crouched over and knees close together—he drilled it into the back of the cup. *All square.*

I was striking the ball well. Then on both seven and eight, I missed short birdie putts. The psychological knife twisted in my gut. After the second one, Bondy imitated Auric Goldfinger: "I expect you to die, Mr. Bond."

Kill him quickly or you'll see him again.

Still *all square.*

It's hard to describe why this mattered so much, but it did. We loved to work together. Being partners in business brought great results and tons of laughter. But in golf, we needed to beat each other. We didn't bet money. We didn't care about our scores—it was all about who would win the match. We were just two primeval boxers trading punches until one fell. This was Scottish golf.

A chance to beat him was unusual. I was nervous as hell. Bondy knew it. And like a brother, he knew what buttons to push.

Upon reflection, the beauty of match play with Bondy was that the competition was all-encompassing. He didn't just live in my head—he partied there with reckless abandon.

Only with total focus could I quiet him. I was forced to think of the match and nothing else. The only thing that could take me out of this zone was allowing him back into my overactive brain. To succeed against Bondy,

I had to learn to tune out his calculated humor—or at least not allow it to affect me. It took time.

At my best, nothing else existed; nothing else mattered. I could hear his funny lines, remember them, but let them pass harmlessly.

Bliss.

The Ruling

Still *all square*, with 170 yards to the pin on the strongly downwind fifteenth, I chose a seven iron. I smoothed it. Straight at the pin. Oh, did that feel good. I held my pose while I watched the ball disappear over the small rise guarding the green. My shot was good. I knew it. Bondy knew it. Flustered, Bondy hit an average shot that would require two good putts to get his par.

Feeling great now, my bag weighed nothing. I came over the small hump and didn't see the ball. Was it possible? I casually glanced at the cup as I walked by, hoping not to be seen doing this. Empty.

Typical of a links, the ball had landed at the front of the green and bounded forward like an excited puppy. The ball rested on a hill about twenty yards past the green. Although we had played the first fourteen holes in well under two hours, I took my time on this shot. I pulled out my trusty 56 degree sand wedge and practiced several times. The shot. Catching it clean and crisp, I loved it. I watched the ball in slow motion as it left my club floating towards the cup. The entire world slowed down. I enjoyed every extended moment.

Out of nowhere, disaster struck. The ball landed in a sprinkler head hole and stopped dead, just off the green.

Having played golf for only a few years, I asked, "What do I do? How do you rule that one? Do I take it over?"

With a sly grin, Bondy responded, "Rub of the Green."

Raising my voice a few decibels, I asked "What? What does that mean? What does Rub of the Green mean? Is that like a let in tennis? Do-over?"

"Rub of the Green means Rub of the Green or that's the way the cookie crumbles, or, in your more vulgar American language, tough shit."

My hat took flight. I stumbled to a seven on that hole.

Lost *one down*.

That Christmas, Bondy gave me a framed booklet cover page from *Rules of Golf* by The Royal & Ancient Golf Club. It reads:

<u>RUB OF THE GREEN</u>

Rule 19. Ball in Motion Deflected or Stopped.

19-1. By Outside Agency. If a ball in motion is accidentally deflected or stopped by an **<u>outside agency</u>**, it is a **<u>rub of the green</u>**, no penalty is incurred, and the ball shall be played as it lies.

CHAPTER II

~

BACK TO THE BEGINNING

Bondy taught me how to play golf. His way. Fast. Competitive. All-consuming. Respectful of the rules and each other. For the last 25 years, almost every time I've stepped on the tee box, I've imagined him saying, "Here's one for the memory banks. Play well, but not too well." No one could make me feel as alive as Bondy when we teed it up.

I took a rather circuitous route to becoming Bondy's primary golf opponent.

I was born in 1960 in Newark, Ohio. My town was a bit larger than Bondy's but with a similar mix of industry and farming. His town had great golf courses. Mine didn't. I was the fourth of five kids with an incredibly hard-working mother and father. My older brother looked like Clark Gable and was one of the most athletically gifted kids in town. My little sister was a national class swimmer. I had large crooked teeth and glasses. I spent a lot of time reading the encyclopedia. I got good grades.

After my freshman year of college in 1980, I took a few years off. Many college students head off to find themselves. I found myself at the local army recruiting station. Iran was holding American hostages in our embassy in Tehran. While my fraternity brothers returned to campus, I marched up and down the muggy streets of Fort Jackson, South Carolina. I loved almost every aspect of Fort Jackson...except the snakes. Soon after basic training, I was sent to Germany to the First Infantry Division (The Big Red One). The army got a great soldier. But I got, by far, the better part of the bargain. I matured. I served my country. I lived and worked with people from all segments of society, many of whom would never have the chances in life I had taken for granted as a freshman in college. My enlistment ended too quickly.

When it was over I went back to college then law school. Got Latin and Greek words with my degrees. School was pretty easy after the army.

After graduating from the University of Michigan Law School in 1988, I joined the multinational law firm Latham & Watkins. I could handle hard work. After the army, I could certainly deal with being yelled at. I would be fine as a highly compensated, but miserable, corner-office lawyer someday.

That's what I told myself, but an epiphany occurred in the closing room on a mega deal that was all over the press. This room was the epicenter of 1980s dealmaking.

One of the firm's partners gleefully exclaimed, "Isn't this deal unbelievable? It doesn't get any better. What a rush. Where else would you want to be?" Despite the huge, dark bags under his eyes, his intensity spoke volumes.

His words conjured images in my mind: thirsty laborers being whipped as they dragged rocks across the desert to build the pyramids. Everybody loved the final result— except the laborers. Self-preservation willed my mouth to utter, "Yeah, that was great." My nose grew as I spoke. With an Edvard Munch scream going off in my mind, I thought, "Are you f—ing kidding me? I'd rather be sitting in a dentist's chair."

I was in the wrong job.

I should have known this would happen when my father wanted me to work at his law firm the summer before law school. Instead, I chose to be a bricklayer's assistant and sold tee shirts out of the trunk of my car.

Most people hated being in the army. I relished it. But as a lawyer, I was an interloper, spending vast amounts of time doing something I hated. Living out someone else's dreams for me. I needed to find a career that gave me as much of a thrill as this deal did for the law partner.

To quote Bondy, "Build the memory banks...there are no mulligans." Don't waste the short years you've got.

So how do you tell your lawyer father that after three years of law school tuition you are taking a 70% pay cut to sell bicycle handlebars?

From Europe.

I moved to Germany in 1991 to sell handlebars. We attacked the market relentlessly. Our team truly believed that our product was superior. We made ourselves the best friends of every shop in which we sold. And it paid off. They loved selling our stuff. We wound up with a leading market share in almost every European country. In 1994, Wilson Sporting Goods hired me. Same strategy. Worked again.

PICKING UP GOLF

My job at Wilson involved sales and marketing for both tennis and golf. Selling market-leading Wilson tennis was easy. But I was somewhat bored with tennis, having played in college. With the golf market growing in my sales territory, I decided to follow Bondy's "suggestion" and learned to play with the small white ball.

Golf, for me, had not been love at first sight.

In August of 1994, two months before I met Bondy, my friend George and I went to the Ring of Kerry with our families for a long weekend. He wanted to play a course called Ballysomething. Although I had played golf a few times on some muddy fields turned into golf courses by local farmers, I was not a golfer. Case in point, six years before I joined Wilson, my rehearsal dinner was at Oakland Hills. It didn't even occur to me to ask the father of the bride if we could play. Instead, we went to see a ball game at old Tiger Stadium.

We left the hotel in Killarney in the morning with the sun shining brightly and the temperature in the low 60s. My friend brought his clubs with him. I didn't own any. I borrowed a heavy, imitation-leather Tour bag, replete with clubs and four dozen balls. I already had a tennis shirt, a cotton sweater, some khaki pants, and a Cubs hat. No one mistook me for a visiting touring pro. Oh, and in case it got wet, I had a Barbour jacket. Yes. A waxed Barbour field jacket. I had no business being where I was about to be.

We showed up. I read the sign. It was Ballybunion. From the clubhouse, I looked outside: "This doesn't look that hard. I don't even see any trees." We paid our green fee. I bought a Coke and a candy bar. Bring on this new sport. I was ready to go.

Some poor caddie drew the short straw and was handed my bag. There may have been a high-tipping, low-handicap oilman checking in just before me...or Ben Crenshaw right after me. But no, he drew a guy carrying a Barbour jacket...one who had made par a few times on short par-threes...if you didn't count lost balls.

From the uber-modern clubhouse, we opened the door and made our way to the first tee. A blast of wind immediately rocked us. Holy—. The dunes were bigger than any hill between Columbus and Indianapolis. The three-foot-tall grass whipped violently, seemingly in all directions at once. What from a distance had looked like a benign version of the moon now felt terrifying. This was dangerous territory. Somebody was going to get hurt.

The exposed first tee had a 30-plus mph wind blowing from left to right. Off to the right sat a graveyard, Celtic crosses and all. I boldly grabbed my driver and took a few practice swings. Satisfied, I reached deep, swung hard, and blasted one. Solid contact. It went dead straight...for the first ten yards. Then, as if laser-guided by the tombstones, it rose in the air with strong sidespin and took a ride in the wind. We never saw it land. But it went right of right. My caddie said nothing. He reached into the bag and handed me a five iron. It didn't matter. Same swing. Same result. Utter silence. My friend, who actually knew how to play golf, suggested I drop one from 150 yards. Sensing the truly horrific potential of this day, my caddie numbly nodded his head.

To make matters worse, I had put all four dozen balls in the bag. The bag wasn't light. My swing made it heavier by the minute. We dropped a fresh pellet near George's ball. George hit a nice one to the back of the green. He had been a high school hockey player. They hit a puck with a stick. Of course, he was going to hit a few good golf shots. But I'd figure it out over the next few holes.

Then it started to rain. The rain stung on the back of my neck. I put on my Barbour jacket. Try swinging in one of those. Humor me. Put the book down. Put a Barbour jacket on. Take a few swings. Even for good golfers, it's hard. Think of those pictures of Jones and Hagen playing in coat and tie. At least they weren't dumb enough to play in a waxed coat made for shooting pheasant in Scotland or pub crawling in London. Now picture a high handicapper, in howling wind, trying to pull off this feat. With knee-high rough on both sides. Let your heart go out to my quickly aging caddie.

On the second tee, the coat helped. The bulk of the jacket prevented me from getting my five iron all the way to the ball. I topped it. It scooted away in shame but ran a reasonable distance down the fairway. On my next shot, I hit one into the deep, deep right hay. Maybe, because we were only on the second hole, or maybe because my caddie took immense pride in his job, we went looking for it.

Bad idea. The moisture from the tall grass immediately soaked up the legs of my cotton pants. What was I going to do if I found the ball anyway? At least I knew enough not to force others to help me look for the ball. They continued, having problems of their own. I picked up.

A few holes and half a dozen balls later, I had my first encounter with those small round bunkers with horizontal lines on the faces. From a distance, to a novice, they look benign, maybe even elegant, in that they are perfectly round with little strips of sod creating the walls. On my first visit, they weren't so harmless; they were deep and nasty. But there was a benefit: the face of the bunker was so high it temporarily shielded me from the incessant pelting of rain.

Four hacks at the ball. Back in the pocket. Upon exiting the bunker, I decided to use my umbrella. That was another error in judgment. The gale-force wind immediately ripped it up. The Ballybunion weather that day could match any wind tunnel created by Chicago skyscrapers.

By now, I had resorted to hitting a tee shot, an approach shot, and maybe a putt or two per hole. But on the eleventh tee, nature's strong wind counteracted my slice. The resulting accident resembled a golf shot.

Number eleven—which I later learned was one of the best holes in the world—stretched down a wild ravine, with large dunes framing the left side and the ocean to the right. Two huge swales interrupted the fairway, creating a virtual minefield of undulating grass. The green was isolated, almost as if it were an island.

As we approached my ball that was a mile from the green, the shocking beauty inspired me. It's hard to imagine what my caddie thought of what transpired next. I decided to take off my Barbour jacket and have a real swing at the ball. Let the athlete out. Dutifully, my caddie held my jacket. Playing for a slice, I aimed my three wood thirty yards left. I crushed it. I *actually* did. The ball made a sound like a bottle rocket as it left my club. Dead straight where I was aimed. It never left its line and buried itself somewhere deep in the dunes. In maybe his only words of the day, the caddie said, "F—*ing* well struck. Really wrong direction, but f—ing well struck. I'd stop after such a good shot." He was right.

I paid the caddie for the full round plus a tip and let him go in early with my bag. I had hit enough balls. He had seen enough bad golf to last a few generations. He didn't need to be asked twice. We made an agreement. I wouldn't say he went in early. He wouldn't talk about my golf. I doubt he held up his end of the bargain. Don't blame him.

27

I walked the rest of the course, honestly believing I had played my last round. Ever!

All that changed when I realized that golf would be a huge part of my business life. After Bondy had teased me about my swing and sent me a copy of Donald Steel's *Classic Golf Links*, he suggested I call the Wilson Tour rep. I learned a grip. I learned a proper takeaway. At work, I continued to hit Wiffle balls every day in my wide hallway. At home, I devoured the book.

My one-year-old daughter didn't know what was being read to her. *Pat the Bunny...Classic Golf Links...The Runaway Bunny...To the Linksland...Goodnight Moon...Classic Golf Links.* We traded on and off. For a while, I had her thinking she was Princess Ailsa from a magical kingdom called Turnberry.

I was hooked.

CHAPTER III

WHITE OUT

On a frigid and rainy February day in 1997, our team gathered at our dreary golf assembly plant in Irvine, Scotland.

In addition to Bondy and me, our team included a vitriolic Frenchman, a highly rational Finn, and an elegant low-handicap Spaniard. The prototypes for a new set of irons, called Fat Shafts, had just arrived. They were cosmetically challenged but had an amazing technology that made mishits fly straighter. As might be expected from a company that wasn't performing well in this category, the product was being rushed to market. Worse, the production forecast was due the next day. If the Wilson tennis division said they had the greatest new racquet, we would assume they were right. Not golf—at least, not yet.

Having seen prototypes months before, but never having hit them, we knew only the theoretical benefits. Our French product manager kept talking about the R&D testing results. But we had heard this BS before. I placed pressure on our team about this product launch: "Has any-one hit them?"

No.

"Golf has thrown a lot of spaghetti against the wall," Bondy responded. "Not much of it has stuck."

I turned, "Bondy, what are your thoughts? If the Fat Shafts aren't home runs, should we allocate the money to tennis?" in other words, to Germany or France. To say this to Bondy and the golf team, I might as well have pulled the pin on a grenade.

Bondy's steely eyes swept the room: "Somebody should hit 'em before we send in the forecast."

They all averted their eyes. Nobody wanted to make direct eye contact for fear of being sent out in this weather. The Spaniard recoiled. At his home course of El Prat in Barcelona, golfers ordered paella on a special phone from the course. It would then be waiting, piping hot, when they came in. Different golf. The cold didn't bother the Finn, but he didn't play well enough. The Frenchman wouldn't tell us the truth.

As I looked around the room, Bondy and I caught each other's eyes and nodded. He said, "OK, let's go. These irons will be tested by a wily old Scotsman and a young guy from Ohio, who is going to be bothered by this cold and lose three and two...then he might be in a bad mood and cancel the entire launch."

As he exited the room, he turned back and winked at the international trio: "I might have to give him a few putts to keep these irons alive."

We made our way through the cold rain to our tiny rental car. When we opened the car door, the wind slammed it shut—not once, but three times. Finally, Bondy stood in front of it while I piled things in the back seat. The trunk was too small to fit clubs.

During the four-minute drive to Western Gailes, we hit defrost twice to clear the windshield. We discussed just playing a few holes. We would likely finish at the seventh, which had a convenient turning spot to go back to the clubhouse.

THE COURSES

The Ayrshire coast of Scotland boasts possibly the finest assortment of golf courses on a small strip of land anywhere. And conveniently, it also housed our distribution center and factory. On the coast, seven courses sit next to each other, three of which rank in the *Golf Magazine* World Top 100. From our factory roof, we could hit a ball onto a course then play seven consecutive rounds, jumping from one excellent links to the next. Better yet, when I was learning to play golf, we would frequently work a full ten-hour day and play eighteen holes after work...provided we played fast. Links heaven.

As with movies and actors, each of the Ayrshire courses has a distinct personality. Turnberry is George Clooney and Brad Pitt. It is great-looking, big-budget, and full of substance. If Cary Grant, an old-fashioned leading man, is your hero, try Prestwick, which hosted the first twelve Open Championships. Hitchcock fans would choose Royal Troon for sheer terror with a classic feel. Western Gailes is Woody Allen: quirkiness with intimacy. Rodney Dangerfield personifies Glasgow Gailes, Barassie, Loch Green, and the Darley course, as they "don't get no respect."

Easily the most spectacular, Turnberry is a true championship links, with its famous white lighthouse, hilltop hotel, cliffside holes, and view of Ailsa Craig, a huge rock formation off the coast. Turnberry deserves its adulation and top twenty world ranking. A quick glance at Turnberry's champions confirms its worthiness: Tom Watson in the famous 36-hole duel over Nicklaus, Greg Norman, Nick Price, and, sadly, not 59-year-old Tom Watson. As to the cost, if you feel compelled to order single malts and cigars or have laundry done, pay cash before your Depression-era father sees the bill.

Quirky, old-fashioned Prestwick, designed by Old Tom Morris, is the birthplace of The Open Championship. Blind shots, funny bounces, and members in plus fours abound. The grand stone clubhouse is a living museum, celebrating golf's hickory and gutta percha days. Tweed-jacketed members drink warmth back into their chilled bones. Some appear to have settled into their worn, leather chairs in the '50s and awakened after Brexit. If they don't leave the club grounds, they won't notice any change.

Royal Troon is a brute but is eminently fair. One of the toughest holes is the eighth, a very short, 123-yard hole called Postage Stamp. On the par-four eleventh, the wind usually blows everything but a well-struck ball onto the adjoining railroad tracks. Bondy once gave me a 75-yard gimme for a ten to win the hole. He said, "That's good—yer hole. Number eleven has seen enough of us." In the Marine Hotel, adjacent to eighteen, you might find Tony Hercus, an insanely knowledgeable malt whisky bartender—just ask him. Sit at his bar for a few hours and the world of whisky opens up.

I could play any of those three courses exclusively and retire from golf a contented man. But for my money, nothing beats the setting and intimate feel of Western Gailes. The charming, red-tiled clubhouse is nestled amongst the dunes, girded by holes that stretch along the coast. A links clubhouse, as it is meant to be.

The first hole satisfies two great links requirements: relatively short and wide open. The driving range is a bar, and the word "mulligan" doesn't exist in Scotland. The first also provides complete refuge from civilization after hitting the tee shot. Pass through the two dunes in front of the tee and all cares but the current round of golf are washed away.

With stunning views of the dune-swept course through the picture windows, the Smoke Room provides a natural transition from the locker room to the golf course. Sturdy oak chairs, well-worn by generations of Western Gailes golfers, are arranged around tables. A few members seem permanently affixed to their seats at the corner table. They occasionally brave the elements to play a seven-hole loop.

My personal favorite was 80-something-year-old Ian MacCleod, nicknamed "Cloudy," presumably, but not definitively, because of his name. I played with Cloudy once early on a weekend morning. Not to be impolite, I drank a few with him before venturing out in the crisp air. My swing was never smoother. I have vague memories of losing on the eighteenth. After the round, Cloudy bought lunch. I bought drinks. As a Scot, Cloudy knew the winning side of that transaction.

At Western Gailes, many members arrive in coat and tie and proceed to the bar for insulation from the weather. They then change into golf attire. Post round, they shower, put on coats and ties, then rejoin Cloudy and the regulars in the Smoke Room to discuss the finer points of the day's round. Bondy joked, "For them, it's then home to a dinner of hot tongue and cold shoulder."

THE MATCH

The club manager was startled when Bondy called: "In this weather, you must be crazy. Come on over. I just might be able to squeeze you in...tee sheet is pretty full." We arrived at a completely deserted Western Gailes and sat down with him for a steaming-hot bowl of Scotch Broth. We then put on every piece of clothing available, including bright red Wilson rain suits. Looking like two Santa Clauses with clubs bundled on our backs, we labored to the first tee, waving at the incredulous club manager. He knew we'd be back after a few holes.

Bondy and I readied to tee off; he agreed to give me four strokes. As I leaned over to put my tee into the hardened ground, it broke. Bondy quipped, "Here's one for the memory banks...cancelled the new irons...young Mr. Reese broke all his tees before he ever hit a shot."

Onward.

Standing on the picturesque seventh tee, I was three up and loving these new irons. Three down, Bondy wasn't sold. Although uncomfortable with a lead against Bondy, I greatly preferred that to trailing. With the match in full swing, we had forgotten about testing the irons. Beating each other had risen to the fore. We also completely abandoned any thought of turning back after seven holes. We weren't even cold.

From the elevated tee box, we paused to admire the vast dunesland ahead with the sea to the right and the clubhouse to the left. Breathtaking. The green is well-protected on the left side by a dune the height of a small castle and pot bunkers that form a moat around it. The massive front right bunker dominated our field of vision from the tee and encouraged us to hit anywhere but there.

My shot flew 175 yards and about two stories up the side of the hill on the left. It burrowed into the tall grass. I needed a fire engine ladder to get to it. I missed on my first swing. Missed again. Somehow, I hacked it out, and it dribbled down to the green. Lying four.

Bondy's tee shot found the massive target bunker that I had so artfully avoided. He temporarily disappeared in the deep cavern. Somehow, a ball came flying out and landed on the green in two. Comically, I rammed in a long miracle putt. Routine double bogey. Bondy dropped his head in disbelief, then three-putted for a half to stay *three down*. After nine, the score remained the same. This was too easy. I started to feel sorry for Bondy, who looked cold and miserable.

Big mistake.

There was no room for compassion with Bondy as an opponent.

Of course, I lost a bunch of holes in a row.

By the fourteenth, we were *all square* and had turned back into the wind. Shit.

Bondy commented how much he liked these new irons. I grumbled about lack of feel.

The usually awe-inspiring view of the clubhouse and the rugged dunesland and sea was now completely obscured by a hard, driving snow.

Still *all square*, we soldiered on. On sixteen both of us hit reasonable drives. Bondy's was down the left side of the fairway. Mine was a little bit right. We trudged after them, bent over like ancient peddlers, weighed down by snow-covered bags on our backs. Visibility was no more than 50 feet.

In ten minutes, so much snow had fallen that we couldn't possibly find our balls. The entire course was blanketed in snow. We instinctively climbed into a deep fairway bunker to get some protection from the howling wind. The snow kept coming. For what seemed like hours—but was probably only minutes—we lay flat on the ground, facing away from each other, too cold to talk.

I thought about ending the match. But I was afraid to show Bondy any sign of weakness. If it stopped snowing, I didn't want him to know I was too cold to keep playing. I looked over at his face. He seemed preoccupied. I suspect he harbored the same thoughts.

I looked up at the top of the bunker; the snow swirled against the dark sky. If anything, the weather was actually worsening by the moment. Two of the fiercest competitors ever to be friends looked directly at each other. No words came out. We looked away, figuring out the next moves in our mental chess match. Neither could imagine giving the other an edge.

Then we looked back at each other. Simultaneously, the words *"All even?"* and *"All square?"* passed through our chattering teeth. We shook hands, laughed with relief, and climbed out the bunker.

Making the trudge back to shelter, I'm sure we resembled Sir Edmund Hillary willing his last oxygen-deprived steps up Everest. Finally, we reached the comfort of the formerly red-roofed, now completely white, clubhouse. Remembering our etiquette, we deposited our snow-covered bags outside and climbed out of our crinkly rain suits. The club manager stood on the warm side of the door holding two glasses of whisky for us. Bondy's lips were so cold, he could barely stammer, "Never hidden in a bunker in a snowstorm...certainly one for the memory banks. Thank you for the wee dram." I nodded in assent. We drank appreciatively.

Back in the office, the rest of the management team had watched in amazement as the snowstorm developed. Most of them had expected us to come back to the office complaining it was too cold to try them out. When we finally returned, everyone anxiously awaited our report on the new irons.

Of course, Bondy recapped the entire round, including our last drives before we climbed into the bunker. Eventually someone reminded him about the irons. "Oh! I forgot. Two thumbs up. But we never would have found Mr. Reese's ball on sixteen."

CHAPTER IV

∼

A COURSE RENAMED

As we snaked our way through the vividly green countryside of Kent a few months later, Bondy regaled me with stories of his nine-day vacation in sun-drenched Portugal. "Went with three longtime golfing friends and our wives to the Algarve for a wee spring tune-up."

He recounted, throwing in local vocabulary with flair, "Finally some warm air, *piri piri* chicken, and Portuguese *rosado*...oh, and lots of practice with the short game. Bad news for you, I'm afraid."

Portugal sounded great.

But the image of Bondy playing nine straight days haunted me. He'd be able to make an up and down left-handed. It was still snowy back home in Munich. Golf existed only in my *Classic Golf Links* book. Serious rust on my game. Despite my golf-less hibernation, Bondy would have no sympathy. I didn't think I was doomed. I knew it.

The English Countryside

Despite my concerns about our impending matches, I soaked in the prototypical English atmosphere during the two-hour drive from London towards the coast, near the White Cliffs of Dover. The Kent and Sussex countryside exemplified idyllic Old England, in stark contrast to Bondy's rough and tumble Scotland.

The area crawled with proper ladies and gentlemen hosting weekend-long casual parties. All things appeared calm and unstudied. New Yorkers in the Hamptons could never pull this off. Somebody would talk about the cost of a party planner. At every junction in this corner of the world, reasonably fit people, wearing Barbour jackets and wellies, walked their Spaniels and Labradors. And although sold separately, Range Rovers did not appear to be optional.

This stretch of South East England is the home of several clubs that fit hand in glove with the London "upper-class weekend" motif. Royal St George's, which has hosted several Open Championships, is the granddaddy of them all. At Royal St George's, with its insider feel, a person senses the presence of unwritten rules. One, which is quite clearly written, prohibits four ball matches. Go out as a twosome or play alternate shots. The members prize speedy play in addition to understatement.

Rye, Littlestone, Prince's, and Royal Cinque Ports round out the group of links courses along this great stretch of coast, with The Open having been held at the latter two. Bondy relayed, "Royal Cinque Ports and Royal St George's are elite clubs called 'Royal something' by the world and a simple nickname—Deal and Sandwich in this case—by members and a small world of English insiders."

For the weekend, Bondy said, "We'll play a best two of three matches in the inaugural South East England Match Play Invitational. I'll likely retire the trophy when young Mr. Reese doesn't show up for year two." We had chosen to play Littlestone, Royal Cinque Ports, and Prince's.

Unlike in the US, visitors can play most top golf courses in the UK on certain days for a guest fee. These fees, plus relatively low maintenance costs, keep the price of membership at reasonable levels.

FIRST MATCH

Littlestone. With a red-brick water tower and huge ship's mast bookending the eighteenth hole, Littlestone embodies old-fashioned seaside golf. Designed before the turn of the twentieth century by W. Laidlaw Purves, who also laid out Royal St George's, it was reworked after the Great War by the famed Alister MacKenzie.

As we got to the first tee, Bondy pointed to the solitary tower in the distance. "Here's one for the memory banks...likely young Mr. Reese jumping from that tall tower after losing in the first and only South East England Championship..."

On that first day at Littlestone, Bondy came out swinging and never let up. For the most part, I made hard pars or bogeys against his easy ones. He struck the ball confidently and dead straight. I didn't stand a chance. We both knew it.

Standing *one up* on the seventeenth tee, Bondy said, "You know, Alister MacKenzie was a fellow Scot. The Boer War influenced his designs." Bondy waltzed in my head. "He put a lot more danger up there than you can see."

My mind filled with images of hidden bunkers. *Where were they?*

He defeated me *two and one.*

That night, we stayed at the Bell Hotel in downtown Sandwich, a beautiful old village. The town came straight out of a Dickens novel, with its timbered walls, irregular reddish-brown roofs, and seemingly dozens of chimneys sticking out of every house. Even in my sour mood, I could feel its charm.

After checking in, Bondy bounded up the stairs, with his feather-light luggage, like a happy teenager. I banged my heavy bag against my shin trying to open the door. An excellent Dover sole, accompanied by a bottle of Sancerre, provided some respite from the day's match. Glad to be playing again after a long winter's break, I dreamt of golf that night. Unfortunately, I dreamt of chipping to fifteen feet. Not restful. Coddled by an opening round victory and a few wee drams of single malt, Bondy slept like a sack of potatoes.

DAY TWO

Our first course for the second day was The Royal Cinque Ports Golf Club, which got its name due to its vicinity to the five military defense ports built by Henry VIII in the 1500s. Bondy relayed, "Naming the Five Ports *Cinque* Ports reminded the French that the English were ready for them."

Having held The Open Championship in 1909 and 1920, the layout at Royal Cinque Ports renders scoring extremely difficult. On the outward nine, the prevailing wind is at the golfer's back. Unfortunately, many of these greens are impossible to hold unless a short iron is struck deftly. Holes twelve through eighteen are long and play directly into the teeth of the wind. Hit straight drives or be prepared for a lot of walking through nasty rough.

Let me digress...In the early part of the century, upper-class members viewed golf professionals in the same light as carnival barkers and vaudeville actors. As such, the golf professionals playing in the 1920 Open at Royal Cinque Ports were not allowed in the clubhouse. Never one to be stymied by rules and regulations, especially those inhibiting his full enjoyment of life, Walter Hagen had his chauffeur-driven vehicle parked directly in front of the clubhouse. To the shock and dismay of the members, his driver then proceeded to serve him champagne and lobster. In the vehicle.

THE MATCH

Bondy and I showed up bright and early at Royal Cinque Ports only to find the clubhouse and pro shop closed. A polite assistant pro collected our green fees and let us be the first group to tee off. Because I had not had anything to eat or drink, I was concerned—only had a half bottle of water from the previous day.

Remembering my drill sergeant's words that the army crawls on its stomach, I seriously considered waiting the fifteen minutes for the pro shop to open. Where was Hagen's limo when I needed it? No lobster. No eggs. No bacon. The desire to play fast won over the need for some food. Ignoring my drill sergeant's advice, I marched to the first tee to join Bondy.

As Bondy skulled his first two wedges of the day, I snidely remarked, "Inside every wedge, there's a three iron dying to get out." For some reason, Bondy didn't find that amusing. I made pars on both holes. *Two up.*

Winning the first two holes made me forget hunger or thirst. I reveled in the smell of the salty air and the chirping of swallows. Bondy was going to have trouble today.

On the par-five third hole, Bondy and I each hit great approaches into the blind punchbowl green.

As Bondy went over the hill to the green, I stopped to adjust one of my golf bag straps. Rounding the corner, I saw Bondy standing next to a ball some thirty feet from the hole. The other one rested only six feet from the cup. My heart skipped a beat. I had a good chance to take Bondy to three down. Bondy's head slumped dejectedly. Rubbing it in, I took my time, carefully setting my bag towards the next tee. I methodically fixed a few pitch marks on my way to my ball—so close to the cup.

As I reached down to pick up my ball, I noticed the telltale player number 7. Yes, as in 007, Mr. Bond. I'd been had. A huge grin exploded on Bondy's face as he jauntily walked towards his ball, next to the cup. "It would appear that you're away, Mr. Reese." Flummoxed, I three-putted. Back to *one up*.

Having been duped by Bondy made me acutely aware of my starvation and dehydration. I would have happily eaten one of those loud birds I had previously enjoyed hearing sing.

Then the wheels fell off.

By the eleventh hole, I was *four down*. Each Bondy up and down increased my thirst. My whining provided all the sustenance he required. With the stupid straps of my ridiculously heavy golf bag grinding into my shoulders, I would have happily climbed into a golf cart—and I hate golf carts.

Despite my dire straits, losing without putting up a fight ran counter to my nature. I dug in. Try as I might to rally, Bondy kept up the pressure. As my hunger and thirst grew, fairways thinned, pot bunkers deepened, and the cup shrank. Every shot played uphill, into the wind with an uneven stance. In contrast, Bondy played downhill and downwind from great lies.

Not a winning formula.

Winning the fifteenth, Bondy beat me by a huge margin. *Five and three.* Bondy had whipped me around like a terrier would a chew toy. "*Five and three, five and three, five and three*," I muttered as I numbly played the final few holes that no longer mattered.

THE RENAMING

Back at the clubhouse, while cooks prepared enough food to feed a platoon, Bondy and I went out to the veranda to see remnants of the Battle of Britain. The bullet holes and the plaque with the names of the club members who had given their lives put my loss in perspective.

As we paid our lunch bill, Bondy slid a scorecard across the table to me, unable—or unwilling—to suppress his grin.

Where the old title of the club had read **"ROYAL CINQUE PORTS,"** Bondy had done a little artwork. The new name of the course was:

"ROYAL CINQUE ET TROIS."

ROYAL CINQUE PORTS
GOLF CLUB
Est 1892

Enid Day

Chapter V

~

Enough Heroes

With the card from the renamed *Royal Cinque Et Trois Golf Club* stashed safely in his jacket breast pocket, Bondy contentedly maneuvered his Saab a few miles down the road. We still had one more match to play before we returned to London. Although he had just closed me out in the South East England Match Play Invitational, Bondy was like a wild dog circling a wounded antelope. Ready to close in. I had to avoid that fate at all costs. For the final match, we ventured just past Royal St George's to a club called Prince's. As he drove, Bondy said, "Now, Prince's has a rich history."

Prince's

Prince's held The Open in 1932. For a US professional in those days, the huge time and expense of getting to The Open frequently outweighed the event's prestige. Many did not bother to make the trip. Gene Sarazen did.

With only one Major title eluding him, Gene Sarazen vowed to get his hands on the Claret Jug. For his attempt at Prince's, Wilson invented a special club called the "sand iron." For secrecy, Sarazen kept it upside down in his bag. Using the new club, he clinched his career grand slam.

Knowing the story, I'd brought a 40-year-old forged wedge with me. In the parking lot at Prince's, I gave it to Bondy. He was moved: "I used to put grips on these years ago at the factory. Dropped one of the heads once. Scratched it. Factory manager docked my pay. Never forgiven him."

Acknowledging history, Bondy indicated, "I think this one will hang in my office as a wee reminder of the South East England Championship. You might need more than a new wedge this afternoon. Maybe a bottle of water and a bag of crisps. I know you don't like to be seen pulling a trolley, so I'll put them in my bag for you."

In classic Bondy fashion, he had a story to tell. For some, flying airplanes matches golf for tradition, romance, and adventure. His story brought golf and flying together.

LADDIE LUCAS

A native son of Prince's, Laddie Lucas, was quite possibly the finest left-handed player in UK history. Born in 1915, the son of the club secretary, Laddie grew up playing with several major golfers of the day. While attending Cambridge he captained the golf team and led the British team in the Walker Cup against America. In addition to playing top international level golf, Laddie learned to fly. At the outbreak of WWII Laddie joined the RAF to fight the Nazis. Noble and honorable.

Bondy pointed up to the skies right over the English Channel. I imagined local villagers scanning for daring dogfights, as the outnumbered RAF battled the seemingly omnipotent Nazis. Laddie and his fellow pilots went up against huge odds every day, knowing that the future of the world hung in the balance. The proud British Lion

Enid Day

stood alone. During his daily aerial battles, Laddie scored enough victories to become an RAF ace. But as with anything, the odds catch up with even the best at some point.

One day, Laddie and his Spitfire came out on the wrong side of the ledger. With his plane crippled by Nazi bullets over the Channel, Laddie steered his way back towards English soil. Coming through a slight break in the clouds, he was rewarded with a most welcome sight. Linksland. As a lifetime golfer, he knew it had to be Royal Cinque Ports or Royal St George's and Prince's just to the north.

"It was not yet known as Royal Cinque et Trois, young Mr. Reese," Bondy quipped and continued with his story.

From the air, a links course looks relatively benign and inviting. With no trees fairways appear wider, the rough less menacing. But on this day, the view was lifesaving.

He came out of the next bank of clouds, smoke trailing from his plane, with little or no time to decide if he was going to parachute into the cold English Channel. He then recognized the clubhouse at Prince's. He was born in that clubhouse. How ironic. He was going to die right where he was born. But if he could put it in the fairway, he'd be safe. He'd done it a thousand times.

"You might want to pay attention here, young Mr. Reese. He probably ate breakfast before he got in his plane to fight the Nazis that day," Bondy added.

"This was bigger than any shot in a club championship, bigger than any putt, bigger than any drive he ever hit...he had to put this crippled, smoking plane in the fairway. Then he sees the fairway of the first hole. 'Darn, I hate the first fairway. I always miss that one,' Laddie thinks. Soon his plane came upon the fourth fairway. 'Don't like that one either.' Sure enough, he missed both fairways but managed to get his plane stopped somewhere in deep rough near the fourth."

The next day Laddie received a telegram from famous golf writer Henry Longhurst. It said, "Driven out of bounds again Lucas."

The romance and adventure of the Laddie story conjured up Winston Churchill's words: "Never was so much owed by so many to so few." Misty-eyed, Bondy said, "So, a wee bit of history here, aye…"

I later asked a few people if they had ever heard of Laddie Lucas. Mike Hall, an Oxford golfer, responded, "Aside from his poor choice of Cambridge, quite a gentleman, really. He was a hero in the war. He certainly had flair. He once flew over to France to get champagne for a party that evening. Rather popular, I'd imagine. He managed to keep a very low handicap at Walton Heath and Brancaster (Royal West Norfolk) into his 70s."

After the war, Laddie became a Member of Parliament and went on to write a few books, including *The Sport of Princes*, about his home course, and *Five Up*, on being an Ace in WWII. Bondy recapped, "Solid life. His memory banks would have been pretty full."

THE MATCH

The Laddie Lucas story inspired us both.

I went over another famous Churchill speech in my head: "We shall fight on the beaches, we shall fight on the landing grounds...we shall never surrender..." I looked Bondy in the eye on the first tee and said, "Well, here goes...US Army vs. the British Merchant Navy."

He laughed. We were both ready for battle.

Sticking the tee in the ground, Bondy was jocular as always: "Here's one for the memory banks, final match of the South East England Championship...not quite the drama of WWII."

Off we went.

Every time I stood on a tee box facing a long, thin fairway riddled with bunkers, I imagined Laddie landing his crippled plane. Hitting a drive didn't seem like such a big deal. Calmed, yet determined, I hit fairway after fairway. As we came to thirteen, momentum switched in my favor.

With Bondy starting to fade his shots to the right, I hit my fourth straight green in regulation. I was striking the ball like Sarazen. My putting, as usual, was shaky.

On consecutive holes, I had two short putts that barely went in, both of them doing victory laps around the rim before dropping. As the second putt miraculously fell, Bondy quipped, "So, we're using the service entrance today.

Hope for your sake they don't close that door when you need it most."

His words reinforced what I was thinking: *I may have used up my luck. Just don't let him in my head. He'll go crazy in there.* He pounced on an opponent's weakness with the vigor of a four-year-old ripping into a pink, sprinkle-covered cupcake.

THE PUTT

One up on sixteen, I put my drive in the fairway. Bondy found trouble. I hit to about ten feet from the pin. Bondy missed the green wide right and chipped poorly. He then putted close for a gimme bogey. Only ten feet away, I now had two putts to go *two-up*. My putt ran by the edge of the hole, and to my horror, began to trickle away. It came to rest a little more than two feet below the hole. Good for customer golf but definitely outside the circle of *this* friendship.

Although I knew the answer, I looked at Bondy, hoping against all odds, for a gimme. Silence. When it came to giving putts at the end of a match, Bondy's heart was colder than a loan shark's. He would make his grandmother get out of a wheelchair to putt a two-footer for the win.

Willing my resolve, I walked over to the ball and marked it. I cleaned it with whatever spit my suddenly tight throat could muster. After replacing the ball, I kneeled behind it with a plumb bob to get the line. A slight left to right break. Why did it have to be one of those? I wondered if the strong wind would have any effect. Should I aim outside the hole? I made several practice putts.

Having already lost two matches to Bondy, I needed to salvage some dignity.

I stepped back away from the putt to look at the line again.

Bondy's delight at my discomfort increased by the second. I took two deep breaths and a steady stance over the ball. With my head marginally clear, I was as ready as I'd ever be. As I pulled the putter back, Bondy stepped forward interrupting me: "That's good."

"Huh?" I responded.

"Pick it up. I'm two down," Bondy said again. Astonished, I had never seen Bondy give a putt before. With a huge grin, Bondy cracked, "Wouldn't want to see my boss break down and cry. Not good for my career."

Despite my winning the next hole easily for a *three and one* victory, Bondy retold the Prince's story: "I had already won the South East England Match Play Championship, so I gave my boss a long putt to keep him happy. Besides, we don't need Mr. Reese to think he is yet another hero from Prince's...just because he sank a short putt."

CHAPTER VI

~~~

MIDNIGHT GOLF

A few months after Bondy's successful campaign in South East England, we journeyed to the far western islands of Scotland.

On a sunny June day a few months after, we boarded a small twin prop from Glasgow to Islay. Flying over the Mull of Kintyre and the Atlantic Ocean, my mind swam with anticipation...*Islay*...as in Single *Islay* Malt. On the short flight, Bondy repeated, "The island is pronounced (I LUH). The S is silent, and the second half is not like what a hen does with an egg."

Bondy continued his lecture: "So gentlemen, Islay is a small and sparsely populated island...whisky distillery for every few hundred adults."

A dream location for a golf trip, if you didn't mind playing two or three rounds of golf a day, visiting distilleries, and eating excellent dinners.

Rinse and repeat.

On the left side of the plane, the ocean stretched to America. On the right sat the lunar-like Machrie golf links, with its enormous dunes, stately white hotel, and desolate, but enchanting, peat bog hills. Closing my eyes, I could almost hear the sound of bagpipes over the drum of the small prop engine.

As the plane's hatch opened, our noses filled with the scent of briny sea air, propelled by a swift breeze. In the distance were dark green, peat-covered hills. Directly in front of us lay huge dunes, covered with tall fescue blowing madly in the breeze. Difficult to find a more inspiring view for whisky drinkers with a golfing problem.

The majordomo of the Machrie Hotel threw our clubs and bags into the van. Looking immediately at the course just beyond the runway, one of our companions, a young golfer from Texas, flirted with the idea of hopping the fence and playing his way to the hotel. "We'll be there soon enough, young Tex," Bondy suggested. "Doubt the course is full. You'll get plenty of golf in unless you plan to break the course record...might need a few extra practice swings."

Tex, called Brian David Dillman by his mother, ran our international tennis division. His motto: I didn't come all the way from Dallas to lay up. Whether playing tennis against Stefan Edberg or golf against Angus Moir, the head of our golf division, Tex thought he could hit every shot needed. Occasionally he would. Exhibiting a rare case of impulse control, young Tex reluctantly piled into the van for the two-minute ride to the hotel.

Welcome to Islay in the summer. Love at first sight.

THE PARTICIPANTS

The eight golfers on this trip came mostly from friendships forged at work. Our favorite Finn, Kari Kauniskangas, was my number two at the company. Scotsman Angus Moir ran our golf division. I had worked for Mark Harris during my ill-advised stint as a lawyer in the States. Michel Goubau was our Belgian distributor. The lone, non-work affiliation was my best friend, a German named Goetz.

Bondy and I shared one of the cabins near the main hotel. Knowing Bondy liked a wee dram or two of whisky after a hard day of golf and fried food, I made sure that our cabin had separate bedrooms. I was prepared to deal with the dangers of passive smoking. Not secondhand snoring.

At the time, Machrie was not a "some play golf while others luxuriate in a spa" couples destination. Pure golf. Great food. Our price per day was 60 pounds per person, which included hotel, breakfast, dinner, and un-limited golf. Pull cart rental added a whopping one pound extra per day. Put in perspective, the price for a day at Machrie was the same as two single malts at the Turnberry Hotel.

THE COURSE

The dominant feature of Machrie was absolute isolation from the rest of the world. Although Northern Ireland could be seen across the water on a crystal-clear day, it might as well have been an ocean away. Machrie remained fundamentally unchanged since the days of Old Tom Morris. It was, bar none, the most old-fashioned course any of us had ever played. Half of the drives and approaches were blind: most frequently hit into punchbowl greens. Of the few bunkers on the course, most were as natural-looking as any that existed in the world.

After unpacking and seeing a large crowd milling around the hotel lobby, we did the 100-yard dash to the first tee. We didn't want to get stuck behind some foursome intent on taking its sweet time. When we got to the first tee, there was no sound except the breeze and no structure except the hotel tool shed. No pro shop. No people. Nothing. Two small cut-in-half whisky barrels for tee markers enhanced the view. Scanning the other partially visible holes, we realized we had the entire course to ourselves. Billionaire golf.

It was hard to imagine a full golf hotel in Scotland with nobody on the course. As it turned out, the other hotel guests were ornithologists. Golfers and ornithologists share hotels well. Each finds the other particularly boring and obsessive. I went on a photo safari in Africa with a bunch of ornithologists once. While the thrill-seekers and immature among us watched lions and cheetahs chase down gazelles, the ornithologists in the group filled out their bird books. Not much mingling. Everybody got what they wanted...except the gazelles.

Here at Machrie, we golfers tried to avoid the bushes and were rarely in the tea-room at 3:00 p.m. The ornithologists didn't hold us up on the course and were in bed before we got to dinner. After learning they were ornithologists, Bondy whispered to me, "Not sure what there is to see on Islay. Maybe they're missing seagulls from their bird book?"

Angus Moir

In an exceedingly rare move, Bondy and I would be teammates. Simple reason. Angus Moir. As in former Scottish Amateur champion Angus Moir. Angus grew up on the east coast of Scotland near Royal Aberdeen and Cruden Bay. Nicknamed Angus McFairway in his teens, his golf was a model of consistency. More importantly, he had a nasty tendency to bomb in long putts, especially late in the round. Bondy and I had fallen victim to those on more occasions than we cared to remember. Angus held the course record at a few places, and plenty of clubhouses have pictures of him. Nice psychological edge when playing a match there.

Blessed with an instantly likeable personality, Angus fit perfectly at the posh golf clubs west of London. He was a well-mannered, double-breasted blazer wearing, West Surrey golf type. Angus possessed an effortless, languid swing and always had a nice thing to say. I imagine that Ted Williams' golf swing would have looked like Angus Moir's. (Bondy and I were just stuck being us.) But beware when playing with Angus—there was a match play killer behind that smile. In the US, a guy like Angus would be the club champion at National Golf Links in the summer and Seminole in the winter. As the younger Scot in the group, he reminded us of Bond...but far more James than Allan.

PICKING TEAMS

Angus was a natural captain of one of the teams. Bondy, the other. Bondy looked at me and called me to his team. With the next pick, Angus chose Mark Harris, who actually loved being a lawyer. With the law, he was the safest pair of hands to be found. Not with a putter. Mark found it easier to negotiate a deal among five angry parties than make a five-footer. A medium to low handicap golfer, he was dangerous from 200 yards. Not twenty feet. He changed putters and putting strokes as frequently as some changed their socks.

Angus' next pick was Kari Kauniskangas, occasionally described as a computer with skin. Kari was a fine athlete and one of my closest friends. But as a golfer, Kari was the opposite of Angus and his smooth swing. Imagine a twelve-year-old boy taking ballroom dancing lessons—stiff and awkward, with sweaty palms. Not likely to produce a good result.

Bondy then selected Goetz, an excellent college tennis and soccer player. However, playing most of his golf in Germany did not prepare him for the wind on links courses. He could be counted on to deliver a few net birdies, a few triple bogeys, and a steady refrain of "How could you guys enjoy playing 36 a day?" But compared to Bondy's next pick, Goetz was a veritable metronome of consistency.

"And with our next pick, we'll take Mr. Boom or Bust, the pride of Dallas, Texas. Tex, welcome to the winning team."

Angus then picked the Belgian, Michel Goubau, to whom we gave two shots a hole. Michel played reasonable tennis and skied gracefully. Golf was a different story. Closing down the clubface, Michel hit everything short left with sidespin...unless he topped it. Giving him two shots per hole kept him competitive...at least on short par-threes.

THE MATCH

As there were eight of us, we played team match play. Our two best net scores against their two best net scores on each hole.

As he stuck his tee in the ground, Bondy looked around at the crowd: "Here's one for the memory banks..." He stepped back and took a practice swing, adding, "I presume they'll serve a wee dram of whisky with lunch." Bondy then took a waggle: "I think I'll take a wee victory nap after that." He then hit a low runner down the middle.

On the 319-yard third hole, the wisest play was to almost stop the approach shot at the top of the hill, and then have it trickle down into the punchbowl green. Any ball struck firmly would hit on the downslope and roll too far. On cue, mine did exactly that. Bondy used his putter from 60 yards...it crested the hill...hesitated...then gently dribbled down towards the hole. Tap in birdie.

Missing only plus fours and hickory shafts, we loved playing a golf course not changed since the days of Old Tom Morris. We would stride up a hill to get a view of the green to see where our balls had wound up. Every time we'd both make pars on a stroke hole, Bondy would exclaim, "There's a few net birdies for young Angus to chew on."

Having both played quite well, Bondy and I felt confident of victory over Angus and his team. Although we had gathered the score of our other two teammates, we did not know the results yet. Ever the gamesman, Bondy kept our card well hidden in his jacket while lunch was ordered, pretending not to know where it was.

At lunch, Angus asked if Bondy had the card for our team. Feigning innocence, Bondy checked all of his pockets. Empty. "We must not have been keeping score. We weren't really sure that there was a match," smiled Bondy. Angus, who had been Bondy's close friend for years, knew he was about to get pasted. Finally, with a big flourish, Bondy discovered the scorecard. Let the scoring begin.

The soup arrived as Angus was announcing his team's score on hole number nine. Bondy read our team's score. We were *three up*.

Bondy then ceremoniously put the card away in his jacket pocket. He calmly and deliberately ate soup; Angus just stewed.

After taking turns reading holes ten, eleven, and twelve, we were now *five up* with six to play. The sandwiches arrived. Again, Bondy put the card away and made Angus wait. After the final sandwich quarter was taken, Bondy announced our score on number thirteen. Another hole to our side, we'd won *six and five*. After that, Bondy's protracted announcing of scores became a tradition.

POST-MATCH

Post lunch, two of us knocked out a quick nine. Others took naps or wrote emails. Mark went to his room to negotiate a deal in three time zones.

Just before 6:00 p.m., we placed our order for dinner at 8:30 p.m. then jammed in a quick fourteen holes of alternate-shot golf. After hot showers, we were seated as dinner arrived. That night, we sat in the bar and taste-tested several of the Islay malts. Those may have been the best beds we've ever melted into. We slept the sleep of the truly deserving. Mark Harris, who did not partake in the wine or whisky tasting, read legal documents. Anybody still wondering why I left a law firm to sell handlebars?

LAPHROAIG

On the second day, after a round of golf and lunch, we took a short ride to the Laphroaig distillery. Smoking the barley over a slow-burning peat fire gave the whisky its famous flavor. Standing in the dark, poorly ventilated smoking room, Bondy asked the stoker if we could shovel some peat. The stoker looked at us, incredulous. Bondy explained, "This young man would like to be a Scot. Not possible. Wrong grandparents. The one thing he can do is help Laphroaig taste peaty." Angus sweetened the deal by offering a sleeve of golf balls.

We shoveled for a while.

Enid Day

For years to come, we would be stocking up on the Laphroaig we had a small hand in making. Bondy leaned in, "Doubt our undocumented labor will qualify us for an employee discount."

THE DUEL

Later that evening, the usual banter ensued. Tex made a comment about carrying our team to victory twice that day. Taking exception, Bondy noted that Tex had shot in the high 90s. Tex was not cowed by a small piece of evidence—the scorecard—that countered his positive self-image.

Well past bedtime, this discussion should not have advanced. But Islay malts have a way of extending things. The bartender suggested we settle our differences like real golfers. A few hundred years ago, islanders might have thrown big rocks or tested their skills with claymores. We had other implements of battle: our mid-irons. It was almost midnight.

Within minutes, the assembled group stood on the fifth tee, with one ball per person. We all tossed our one-pound coins into the pile. One shot. Closest to the pin. Winner takes all. The 163-yard par-three was playing into a slight breeze, making everyone cagey about what club they would actually use. Michel went first. Inebriated shouts of "just practice" filled the otherwise empty night air. We agreed not to count his first swing and miss.

I went next. Fat and nasty. Couldn't see it. Didn't matter. Two others followed, and we could make out the faint lines as the balls headed towards the green.

By now, the Tex and Bondy banter would have made Spike Lee and Michael Jordan proud. A few of us reminded Bondy that Tex might actually have the edge. Bondy had a belly full of food, wine, and whisky and a stiff back. In contrast, Tex was about 30 years younger and had played number one singles on a major college tennis team...and Texans drink and shoot things all the time.

As expected, Bondy rose to the occasion. He hit a punchy little five iron into the wind. He gave a fist pump as we all saw the ball head towards the pin. That one would be good. Tex went next and made a smooth swing. None of us saw the ball. He insisted it was a great shot.

Clouds obscured the moon. Midnight darkness. Some could not see clearly anyway. After a fair amount of fumbling around, we found a few balls resting comfortably in the bunkers. Many made a half-hearted look around the green before migrating like shepherdless sheep back towards the warmth of the hotel. A few of us continued searching on the moon-shadowed green.

We spotted the only ball on the green, which was resting in a better lit section, about 30 feet directly past the hole. Tex shrieked, "Yes! I knew I hit a great shot!" However, on close inspection, it was marked with player number 7: Mr. Bond. Imagine Bondy doing a Scottish sword dance at midnight on the green after a few Islay malts. Not pretty. But effective.

Bondy offered to buy the group drinks with his victory earnings. Some took him up on the offer and ordered the best single malts they could find on the menu, dramatically exceeding the seven pounds in the pot. Flush with victory, Bondy didn't care.

The next morning as we were teeing off, Mark spotted something on the fifth green. No more than five feet from the cup, Mark reached down and picked up a small white object that had been obscured by the shadows the night before. There it was. Holding up a ball with the marking "TEX," Mark called out to the crowd, "Hey, Bondy, it looks like you owe Tex seven pounds."

His head drooping, Bondy responded, "There's one to you, young Tex." He dutifully paid him seven pounds.

We all thanked Bondy again for the drinks.

Nobody reimbursed him.

Chapter VII

~

A Most Difficult Par

After two and a half blissful days at Machrie, we settled our ridiculously small bills and gave our livers a reprieve. Letting us off at the water's edge, the hotel's chief steward waved goodbye. Sprayed by an ocean mist on the deck of the boat, we watched the purple-hued hills of Islay recede, not knowing if we'd return. But every time we'd take a drink of Laphroaig, it would bring back fond memories.

Onto our next destination: the equally remote but nearby, Machrihanish.

One of the books in my daddy-daughter story time rotation was Michael Bamberger's links love story, *To the Linksland.* I poured over his descriptions of Machrihanish's natural setting, wild dunes, and faraway location. Not sure how my by-then four-year-old daughter felt, but I longed to play it.

Many golfers only want to go where The Open is played. Fine for them. Our crew had a different view. Being remote added to a course's allure. For us, Machrihanish was worth a journey. It was only about fifteen miles from Machrie as the crow flew. We took a van, then a boat, then a bus, then a taxi.

THE HOLE

The 500 World's Greatest Golf Holes, by *Golf Magazine,* ranked the single best holes by hole number. The list contained many of the usual suspects. The finishing hole at Pebble Beach was the best eighteenth, the Road Hole at St Andrews represented the best seventeenth, and Azalea at Amen Corner the best thirteenth. But the best opening hole in the world is at Machrihanish. If you've got a lot more time than money, go play it.

On a links course, the first hole is frequently just a way to get from the mediocre land around the clubhouse out to the "real" golf country. Machrihanish puts this theory on its ear.

At 423 yards, the first hole is not overly long. But it has one of the most intimidating opening shots anywhere outside of the first hole at Prestwick, which has a railway running down the right side.

The curved coastline that shapes the first hole at Machrihanish resembles the eighteenth at Pebble Beach. But the tee box at Machrihanish juts 30 yards farther out into the ocean. Standing on the tee box, a vast expanse of ocean and beach extends in front of you, with a small crescent shaped fairway just beyond. Fescue-covered dunes frame the inviting green, with purple hills in the distance. The beach starts immediately in front of the tee box and goes further than I can hit.

The right side of the fairway is wide open encouraging cautious players to drive out to the right. But a safe tee shot leaves a monstrously long second shot, playing over greenside bunkers. The bold—or reckless—take on the beach, where success leaves a short iron to the green. Classic strategic golf.

With Angus back home, the remaining seven of us stood on the small tee box overlooking the beach and waited for the first group to tee off. Ever the seasoned match player, Bondy drove well out to the right, playing for a bogey or a great up and down for par. The next two players followed suit with slightly more aggressive lines.

Then came Tex, whose effortless swing would have every unwitting golfer clamoring to be his partner, a conclusion fraught with peril. *Caveat emptor.*

This former top-ranked tennis player's testosterone overflowed. He was a human highlight reel. Good and bad. Tex could be goaded into going for almost any shot no matter how many times he had repeated his pre-round mantra, "I'm going to hit seven iron on the second shot of every par-five." His genetic wiring did not permit a safe bogey when heroic death at the Alamo was available. Bondy knew how to pull those strings.

Bondy, Tex's opponent for the day, remarked, "I had to play safe. Big hitters like young Tex and Angus get to go for it."

His shoulders slightly straighter than a moment before, Tex predictably quipped, "Straight to the green, baby."

It was now a battle of cultures and attitudes. Bondy quietly offered the group five pounds on "world vs. fairway." No takers. Tex took the club back and savaged it. One of the finest drives any of us had seen. But one yard short. Welcome to the Atlantic Ocean.

"That's a bit unfortunate, young Tex," Bondy commented, "A wee gust of wind just held that up. Well struck though. I've never hit a ball that far." Tex was easy prey.

The second shot on number two, up a hill to a blind green, gave access to the wild and wooly dunes à la Ballybunion or Cruden Bay. The meat of the course wound around spectacularly high, fescue-covered dunes, with a slight interruption for a military airfield. Awe inspiring. The finish was less so. Number eighteen had a tee box and a green.

Our two groups cruised around the course in under three hours. We then gathered in the clubhouse, really more of a bar, on the other side of the road. As usual, lunch consisted of toasted sandwiches, soup, and heaping platters of fries. We didn't really need a menu. We vacuumed down superhuman quantities of sandwiches, one quarter at a time, then ambled to the first tee for round two.

This time six of us left the warmth and comfort of the bar to make our way to the first tee, with the Atlantic Ocean spread out before us. Fresh from an easy morning victory over Tex, Bondy decided to rest his ailing lower back. Only a singles match against me might have coaxed him to play.

Our two groups played a quick second round. As usual, I struck the ball well but putted like a dachshund. Coming off the course, we went straight for dinner at the clubhouse bar. Bondy had kept one of the seats warm while watching the weekend's golf on Sky TV.

Over fresh seafood, we effusively praised the course, loving the natural dunesland and remoteness. We couldn't stop talking about number one. A common refrain: "I didn't even come close to parring it." Of course, young Tex started to speak about his par, but was cut off by Bondy: "With the first ball, young Tex. No mulligans in Scotland." Smiles all around.

As a group of reasonably good golfers, we had played it thirteen times. Nobody had made par. Although we had other things going on in our lives, some of us became as obsessive as Captain Ahab on golf trips. The hole could be parred. I looked at Mark. He looked at me. We both looked outside at the slowly receding daylight. Bondy egged us on: "Doubt very many Americans have made par there and certainly no Germans unless Langer flew over here with the Luftwaffe." Instinctively, we knew what was next. Unspoken, we nodded and smiled.

We asked the bartender, "Is it okay if we go out and play number one until we par it?" He skeptically looked outside at the diminishing daylight, then smilingly, over at our table full of empties. "Nae issue," he grinned. "Best of luck to you, lads." He may have augmented his income by collecting bets in the bar against us.

Goetz joined us. After playing 36 and drinks, Goetz swung too stiffly to get any power. At the time of our trip his handicap at his home club in Frankfurt was in the mid-teens, but he couldn't break 95 on a windy links course to save his life. Mark was a nine. I was a twelve. The small support crew in the base camp (the clubhouse bar) shook their heads as we made our way to the first tee. Ever the Scot, Bondy wondered whether we had paid our portion of the bill.

THE CHALLENGE

9:51 p.m. Still reasonably light. Establishing camp at the first tee, we faced a two-club wind and a temperature in the mid-50s. Setting our bags down, we chose only essential gear for the assault, leaving everything else behind on the empty tee box. The pro shop next to the first tee had long since closed. To think we would only be playing this once would be a triumph of hope over experience. On the first attempt, all of us landed safely in the fairway, but well to the right, leaving exceedingly long second shots. Goetz and Mark hit three woods, and I hit a choke down three iron to keep it low. All of us came up well short—30 to 50 yards. Goetz chili dipped; he was out. Mark and I chipped poorly. Neither of us came close to making our putts for par. *Goetz–6, Mark–5, Luke–5.*

10:11 p.m. With the light diminishing, the wind held steady at two clubs into our teeth. The temperature had now dropped into the high-40s. Taking bolder lines on this set of drives, Mark found the middle of the fairway, I wound up a bit to the right. Goetz sent his splashing down on the way to Machrie or Boston, depending on the current. It would take two *really* great shots for Goetz to make par now. Mark and I were still in it. My driver off the deck missed twenty yards left. Mark duffed his second shot but hit his third to fifteen feet. I chipped to twelve feet. We both missed the putts. *Mark–5, Luke–5, Goetz–big number.*

10:27 p.m. Darkness now blanketed the course. The wind had picked up, and the flag in the distance was no longer visible. With a three to four club wind in our faces and the temperature dropping precipitously, we donned wind jackets over our sweaters. All three of us found the fairway with our drives. Mark's well-struck three wood wound up somewhere left of the green. My poorly hit "runner" wormed its way to the green and came to rest 25 feet from the pin. In the darkness, we didn't find Mark's ball. The lights from the bar and the town looked like a little fishing village glimmering off in the distance over water. With a warm Mediterranean temperature and the right companion, this scene would have been enticingly romantic. Instead, I was in four layers of clothing playing a hole for the fifth time that day. Still, no better place to be.

No room for other thoughts, I just had to get this putt really close.

I lined it up and took several practice swings. I made a good stroke. The ball tracked towards the hole and nestled up one foot short. Yes! After five tries each by the three of us, and seven more tries by the other four in the group, (22 attempts in all), we had finally made a par on the best opening hole in golf. Smiles and high fives abounded. I walked up to tap the ball in.

It lipped out.

Bogey.

CHAPTER VIII

~

LOCAL LEGEND

A few weeks after Machrie and Machrihanish, we found ourselves in London for three days of budget meetings. Upon finishing, we rushed through the heathlands to Heathrow and caught an earlier flight.

Sitting in the far back of our packed flight, we felt every bump as the plane began its descent over the west coast of Scotland. It was about four in the afternoon. Angus and I simultaneously looked at our watches. Then at the same moment, we glanced outside and turned to each other. Bondy started chuckling, "You two young lads run around the course. I'll go meet our good friend, the bartender, Tony Hercus. I have to smooth things over...after our reps called him a miserable wanker the last time Neil Parker played the piano too loudly."

Dinner was scheduled for 8:30 that night with the entire sales team. Angus and I refused to languish for two hours in a hotel bar surrounded by links courses.

All the logistics would have to work seamlessly:

Bags—4:45

Rental car—5:00

At Troon—5:40

Tee box—6:00

Off the course—8:15

Showered and at dinner—8:30

Challenge accepted.

The hotel sat about 45 minutes south of Glasgow Airport. In our many journeys together over the years, we have occasionally made it in much better time. Doing so always involves luck and somewhat aggressive passing on a narrow, winding road. Shortly after touchdown, we bolted out of the plane. With Angus hustling to get the rental car, Bondy and I gathered our golf clubs. We had the overstuffed car hurtling over bumpy, rain-slicked roads within ten minutes of landing. Ahead of schedule. Taking cues from fellow Scotsman Jackie Stewart, Angus kept the car redlined. We reached the Marine Highland Hotel, perched over the eighteenth fairway at Royal Troon, with plenty of time to play. Bondy would drop us off at the golf course then go check in.

Our first choice of venue was the front yard of the hotel, the Royal Troon Championship Course. Angus ran in to see the club secretary, who happened to be Colin Montgomerie's dad. The course had just hosted The Open

Championship, so the membership hardly welcomed an unscheduled twosome, even one that included a former Scottish Amateur champ. Angus exited the Royal Troon clubhouse with his head hung low; I started the engine. No Postage Stamp today.

Before he could close the car door, I had the car racing towards Troon's public links trio. The first holes all start in the same spot and head out in the same direction. Good chance we'd luck out here.

When we arrived, it was like a mountain base the first Saturday after a fresh powder dump: swarms of golfers waiting to tee off on each of the courses. No lightning round to be had. Two false starts. Tires screeching, we zipped back to Royal Troon.

As Angus jumped out of the car, Bondy yelled out, "Remind him that you beat his kid in the Scottish Am. Maybe that'll do the trick." Angus shook his head and chuckled. We paid modest green fees to play the Royal Troon Portland course, an under-appreciated Alister MacKenzie track. Although not quite the championship course, it was still fun.

We parked about 50 feet from the first tee. With less than two hours to play, Angus and I hurriedly dumped our bags on the ground and found golf shoes, clubs, worn golf gloves, and a few balls. I gulped a bottle of water and inhaled a candy bar.

Once we felt moderately equipped for golf, we piled everything together and threw it back into the trunk. We would sort out ownership post round. Bondy howled as he drove off, "Get a few extra strokes, Mr. Reese!"

With the temperature at 55 degrees and a slight breeze blowing, we left our heavy, swing-inhibiting rain suits in the car. We were clad in long-sleeve shirts and club-crested, scratchy wool sweaters. Some wives think we have too many of these. No complaints after replacing them with elegant KJUS (pronounced 'shoos') ones.

We fixed our bet, which involved no money.

Our golf bags precariously balanced on our shoulders, we scrambled to the first tee. We would forget about the hectic start within a few shots. Despite the time crunch, we relished a firm links fairway in a slight breeze. Hopefully, our backs would forgive us.

While I tied my shoes, Angus took a few stiff practice swings then hit a rushed tee shot. He topped his shot, but it still ran 220 down the middle of the concrete-hard fairway. I hit my tee shot poorly, but it, too, got some roll. Stepping off the first tee, Angus laughed, echoing Bondy, "No mulligans in Scotland."

Of course, Angus opened with a birdie.

"Nice relaxed warm-up," Angus grinned. He half-jogged to the next tee.

At that point I was playing to a twelve, Angus played off scratch. In the US, that would have made Angus a plus two or three. Some quick key differences. In the US system, they take the average of your ten best scores from your last twenty rounds. In the UK, the handicap is a mathematical average of one's scores during club tournaments. To put it in a different way, an American golfer's handicap is a reflection of what the golfer can be. In contrast, a British golfer's handicap reflects what the golfer is. Note to fellow Americans: don't play match play against a Brit for money.

Angus gave me three-quarters of the difference between his zero and my twelve. (The advantage goes to the better player—that's UK golf.) However, to give me some extra help, he let me use my strokes whenever I wished— even after the hole. In the UK, they call these traveling strokes bisques. I gladly took his charity.

Playing links golf with the former Scottish Amateur champion (and getting only nine strokes) was intimidating but also brought out my best. In a round against Angus years later, I had a four-hole stretch where I went birdie, net birdie, net eagle, and net birdie. But let's remember Angus. He oozed confidence on the course and had one of the smoothest swings around. A birdie never seemed out of reach. I didn't gain any ground in that match.

To top it all off, he had a bag full of match play tricks. All Scots seem to exit the womb ready for savvy match play. Just like Bondy, he trotted out his sly maneuvers when they would inflict the most damage on an opponent. With Bondy, you knew for certain that he didn't mind seeing you hit a really bad shot. He was always quite funny about it, but you knew he was against you. Sort of like an annoying older brother.

But with Angus you got lulled into thinking he was rooting for you. He was your friend and instructor—sort of like my favorite Uncle David. Angus wanted you to strike the ball better than ever—but *just* barely miss your putts. He wouldn't cheapen your relationship by letting you win. He would then comment, "That's unfortunate. Nice roll, though. Wee bit unlucky there. These are tough greens." You were losing, but he made you think you were playing great. And Angus would be on his way to another victory.

Before years of hardening by the different match play approaches of Angus and Bondy, I was particularly susceptible to both. For the first two years or so, I didn't realize that Angus truly wanted to beat a relative beginner. There was never a question about Bondy. The reality was simple. Both Angus and Bondy wanted to win every time they put a tee in the ground.

Scots don't do casual match play.

THE MATCH

On the first three holes, Angus made two pars and a birdie, forcing me to burn one of my bisques to stay *all square.*

On the short par-three number four, I hit my seven iron beautifully. The feeling of an iron striking a ball on links turf provided immense pleasure. The ball exploded off the face, the club making a thumping sound as it hit the sandy turf. As I watched the well-struck ball in flight, a feeling of pure anticipation filled me. On a links course, you don't really know how good a shot is until the ball hits the ground and starts rolling. In this case, it hit just in front of the green, missed a bunker, and rolled up to ten feet. Happy to have a bit of luck.

Angus struck his ball on a perfect trajectory that never left the flag. It hit, rolled, and stopped about two feet from the cup. Angus tapped in for birdie. Again. Despite playing my best possible golf on the first four holes, I had now been forced to use two of my bisques just to keep things *all square.* Bad omen.

As we were playing, we looked out at a vast expanse of rippling linksland, dotted with gorse bushes stretching for miles over several courses. The wispy, brown grass bent heavily as each gust of wind blew in from the sea. The weather was still comparatively benign—our sweaters warding off the dusk chill. To our left, the public Lochgreen course lay beyond the railroad tracks. To our right, Royal Troon's Championship course glowed, bathed in streaks of sunlight coming out of the fast-approaching dark clouds. In the distance we could see the large, hilly dunes that included the treacherous Postage Stamp hole.

On two of the first six holes Angus had doled out generous gimmes, ostensibly for the sake of keeping the match moving along. I was addicted to this pace. I appreciated the camaraderie with such a great golfer, and I admired his gentlemanly manner.

The clouds we had seen over the Championship course now sat directly over our heads. With the temperature dropping sharply and the wind picking up, Angus and I rooted around in our nearly empty golf bags for some protection.

Maybe we had too severely reduced weight before teeing off. A half-eaten banana, six pencils, and four scuffed golf balls were all that kept the two wool caps in my bag company. We each donned a tweed Irish cap that nongolfers find particularly appealing, especially on paunchy middle-aged men. I could only imagine what my daughters Madeline and Olivia would have thought of me in one of these caps. "Dad, you look like the old farmer in *Babe*." Forget appearances. The cap kept my head, with its thinning topside, dry, and it never blew off in a heavy Scottish wind.

Omnipresent grey Scottish clouds began to sprinkle on us, just like Chicagoans on Election Day, who do their business early and often. Being links-golf-crazy, we both smiled, especially with wool caps keeping our heads dry. Soon the familiar scent of slightly damp wool hit our noses. It fit a traditional links course, but most of all, the light rain driven by a cold wind magnified the "playing golf in the elements" aspect of links golf that we both found so cathartic.

We were *all square* on number ten. Angus uncharacteristically duffed his approach shot. I hit my approach to the middle of the green. The door of opportunity briefly opened. I thought I was going to win the hole with an easy two-putt. Angus dashed my hopes by hitting a 60-yard bump and run to one foot. Easy par.

With my plans changing mid-stroke, I took a slightly harder go at my birdie and watched it roll a foot and a half past the hole. As I walked to scoop it up, Angus applied pressure, gently murmuring, "It might be nice to see that one in." After giving me all of those putts early on, I had become dependent on his charity. I wondered how despondent I would feel if I missed. I got my answer. Only four bisques left.

Coming up eleven, I remarked about life in these small Scottish towns, where golfers could play late summer nights. My comments struck a nerve deep in Angus.

The brisk play combined with the nearly perfect conditions—slightly rainy, fresh breeze—opened Angus up.

Golfers are frequently asked, "What do you talk about for eighteen holes?" When we answer, "Don't know," we aren't imitating our young daughters, who share school-day stories with the forthrightness of the CIA—we really don't remember. However, on this day, I remember every detail.

THE LEGEND

Angus was loath to discuss his own Scottish Amateur championship, won in 1984—Colin Montgomerie lost in the semifinals of the other bracket. But when it came to spinning a yarn about Scottish golf, Angus was the "Son of Bondy." Angus relayed to me the story of Bartonholm, a small mining hamlet just north of Troon that had produced three Scottish Amateur Champions. Yes. Three. Its population never reached more than a few hundred, and Bartonholm ceased to exist some time ago.

Hailing from this tiny industrial town, three local Scots had pulled themselves up by their bootstraps and managed to win their country's national championship five times. Think of *Hoosiers* happening in 1937, 1939, 1947, 1961, and 1969. In 1961, Jimmy Walker won at Western Gailes. Jackie Cannon won at Troon in 1969. Saving the most colorful player for last, Angus then told me of a man whose name screamed Scotland: Hammy McInally.

HAMMY

After winning the Scottish Amateur Championship at Barassie in 1937 by a score of six and five, then in 1939 at Prestwick again by a score of six and five, Hammy capped his career at Glasgow Gailes with an outlandish victory of ten and eight in 1947. If victories make up the full measure of a player, Hammy led an incredibly full golfer's life. But his accomplishments only scratched the surface of Hammy as a Scottish golfer.

With a hard-scrabble background, Hammy had little time for the gentlemen golfers permeating the game in the '30s and '40s. In one important Scottish amateur event, Hammy had his opponent dormie—five holes up, with five holes to play. With his opponent in real trouble, Hammy needed only a 100-yard wedge to the center of a huge green to secure victory. Hammy looked at the lie carefully. Mischievously eyeing his opponent, Hammy pulled out his three wood, turned sideways, and blasted the ball out of bounds, saying, "Yer hole" in his thick Glasgow accent. He closed out the match on the next hole. Afterwards, someone asked him about his decision to hit the three wood out of bounds. "Best lie I had all day," he laughed. "Seemed a shame to waste it on a fookin' pitching wedge."

Back in our match, our soggy golf bags were only getting heavier. We walked up the thirteenth fairway crouched low against the cold, rainy wind. Angus continued.

In one foursomes match, Hammy was pitted against a blue-blooded, retired English officer. Scotland vs. England. On the fifteenth hole, with Hammy and his partner one up, Hammy's partner hit his drive deep in the left rough. As the Scots feverishly searched the weeds for the ball, the retired officer pulled out his pocket watch and began to time them. Eyes fixed on the timepiece, he never looked at the ground. As the second hand hit five minutes precisely, he informed Hammy and his partner, "I do believe that the ball must be declared lost." The match ended *all square*. Hammy and the officer did not share a lunch table.

Angus blasted his drive on fourteen, then resumed telling of Hammy and the Officer. As fate would have it, Hammy played the Officer that afternoon in singles. As certain as there is justice in the world, the Officer hit his drive on the same hole deep in the left rough, just where Hammy and his partner had lost their ball that morning.

Unlike the Officer, Hammy took golf etiquette seriously. He looked hard for his opponent's ball. After a long time, Hammy asked, "Excuse me, Senior Officer, sir. You wouldn't happen to have that fancy pocket watch on you by any chance, would you now?"

Mumbling into his chest—the suddenly sheepish Officer answered, "Why, yes, I do."

"Would five minutes have passed then, sir?" Hammy continued.

The officer confirmed that the five minutes of searching for a lost ball had in fact elapsed. Radiating innocence, Hammy pressed on. "Are ya sure it's been five minutes? Because you've got to have the full time."

Reluctantly, the stuffy Officer checked his watch again. Five minutes was well past.

Upon confirmation, Hammy pointed to a nearby spot on the ground and exclaimed, "Good, 'cause there's your fookin' ball."

Hammy won the match easily.

Back in our match, darkness fell quickly. Angus and I could barely hold clubs in our damp, chilled hands. Our drenched wool sweaters, which had admirably resisted the light rain, had long since lost their form. Ducking behind a gorse bush as he swung, I dreamt of dinner.

We would eat like a pack of ravenous wolves that night.

The Final Hole

Angus and I both reached the green in regulation on seventeen. With the course nearly submerged in darkness, we knew this would be our last hole, and with a *one-up* lead and one bisque left, I wanted to make sure that I didn't screw up with a three-putt. Although the steady rain had slowed down the greens, I was pretty sure of the speed. After taking a few practice strokes, I stepped up and hit my 30-footer. It left the putter face hot but slowed as it approached the hole.

As it stopped within easy gimme range, Angus reached out and knocked the ball back. "Your ball striking is excellent," Angus said, "and your putting is definitely improving. You shouldn't get strokes from Bondy anymore."

After his kind words, Angus then took a careful look at his twenty-footer. As he briefly took in the line of the putt and visualized the speed, I imagined Hammy treading these very greens 50 years before. Angus stroked the putt. The ball never left the hole. Dead center. Back of the cup. Just another long bomb from Angus. What else...birdie.

It was too dark to play the final hole. Angus took off his cap, smiled, and offered me his hand. "One more thing: practice hitting 100 two-footers in a row. It'll really groove your stroke."

With that advice, this seemed like the right way to end. *All square.*

When we got to dinner, Angus mentioned Hammy. Bondy briefly paused. "That's certainly a name from the distant memory banks. Let me think. Jack Cannon, Jimmy Walker, great players...but Hammy McInally...he was a character...you know, my father-in-law, Margaret's father, played his golf at Bogside. I think Margaret went to Sunday high tea at the club. They'd all be there."

As might be suspected, Bondy knew far more than Angus about the three champions from Bartonholm. They had been a lot older than Bondy but had grown up near him. That evening, a small crowd clung to each word as Bondy told stories of Hammy.

Aided by some of the Marine Hotel's precious single malts, Bondy filled in many details Angus had not known. After light prodding from Angus, Bondy confirmed our suspicions when he commented, "But let me tell ya, if I've got Luke Reese five down with five to play, don't expect me to hit the three wood out of bounds. I'll step on his skinny neck first, then show off a wee bit. Of course, I would probably wait for a hole and make it 5 and 3... reminds me of a course called Royal Cinque et Trois...have I mentioned this to any of you?" Off he went.

After his second Glenmorangie, it came out that a wispy lad named Bondy had played a round with Hammy in the 1950s.

Bondy recalled, "Hammy crushed me mercilessly."

Chapter IX

Best Caddie Ever

With nobody in front of us, Bondy and I played fast. For the first few holes, the course played up and down the hilly terrain with more than a fair share of blind shots. After the fourth hole, we came to a screeching halt. In front of us, two foursomes played a tournament. As guests, we had no status. We weren't going through anybody. We contented ourselves by practicing our putting on the fourth green. After an eternity, we meandered in the direction of the fifth tee box.

Out of nowhere, a golf ball thumped on the fourth green. Soon another thump. Two balls nestled their way reasonably close to the pin for easy pars. The well-struck balls were chased by two fast-walking, elderly Welshmen...

But I'm getting ahead of myself.

Let me back up.

That morning, Bondy and I had presented the new Wilson tennis collection to a few retailers in London.

It went fast. The only question was "Can we get more than our allocation?" We followed the first rule of sales: once you have the order, stop talking, and get out of there. Suddenly, we had a few hours to kill before we'd planned to meet up with some of my family for a golf trip through Wales. Enough time for an emergency eighteen.

We pulled out a copy of Tom Doak's soon-to-be classic *The Confidential Guide to Golf Courses* to find hidden-gem courses near Swansea. Bondy read Doak's description of Southerndown Golf Club: "Far and away the best 'downland' course I've seen in the British Isles...The clubhouse occupies a magnificent prospect high on the downs above the Bristol Channel, with marvelous views across a long range of dunes toward Porthcawl...Definitely worth checking out if you make it as far as Porthcawl."

"Never heard of downland. Let's play that one," Bondy said.

Bondy phoned a very accommodating golf professional at Southerndown, who indicated, "You might not get in all eighteen. You'll have to pay the full green fee, though." The Welsh can make tightfisted Scots seem like Jay Gatsby throwing one of his lavish parties.

We hurriedly filled the car with road trip necessities and climbed behind the wheel. No time for lunch. Provisions included two Diet Cokes, a few bags of Walkers Salt & Vinegar crisps, and about eight pounds in cash.

Two fugitives, we steered our car due west from London on the M4. Of course, we didn't have directions to the club. Why take an extra five minutes at the office? We presumed one of our two cell phones would be partially charged (in case of an emergency).

After a few hours, we crossed Severn Bridge, the entrance to Wales. At 37 I had sold products all over the world, but had never been to Wales, my family's ancestral home. I looked around trying to absorb all the details. Sort of like England, only less picturesque.

Despite a fair amount of German blood, my father considered himself entirely Welsh. I had heard stories. Nobody discussed what they ate or what our coal-mining town looked like. We were told they had to save money because every few years some terrible event would occur. They left. Got through Ellis Island and eventually settled near a place called...Welsh Hills. Determined? Yes. Smart? Debatable.

We were set to play several classic golf links. We would start with the southern courses: Pyle & Kenfig, Royal Porthcawl, Pennard, and Tenby. Then we would hit Aberdovey and Royal St David's (Harlech) in the middle of the country. Finally, Conwy in the north. The schedule called for us to meet the rest of the group for dinner this evening on the south coast of Wales, about a three-hour drive from our London office.

SOUTHERNDOWN

Southerndown smells of the sea. It plays firm and fast. Gorse bushes abound. The wind blows all the time. No trees. Yet it is not classified as a links.

Despite its proximity to water, Southerndown sits 150 feet above sea level. A links course is traditionally viewed as the "link" between the land and the sea. If you happen to be at Southerndown, pretend you are 150 feet lower. Basically, links golf.

As we unpacked our gear, Bondy looked around for his shoe bag. Nowhere in sight.

"Did you put my shoes in the car?" Bondy asked. "They were on the clubs."

"In the US Army," I smirked, "we carry our own gear."

"I wasn't asking you to pack my gun."

"It's called a rifle," I answered. "A gun is for artillery. Maybe in the Merchant Navy, you dumped each other's things onto the boat. Can't really get left behind there."

"A boat has oars. We sailed on a ship."

Chuckling, we entered the pro shop. Bondy looked for a pair of white shoes but could only find FootJoy Classics. He saw the price and recoiled. Amazing shoes. Stratospheres above his standard Scottish price point.

I walked over to the sale section. "Get these brown ones. On sale."

He looked at me as if I had insulted his mother: "I wear FootJoy. Best brand...and I wear only white saddle shoes. Can I tell you a story?"

"If I said no, would that stop you?"

"You see, young Mr. Reese," he continued, unabated, "Seve Ballesteros wore white shoes. Some say that he would move his legs while his opponent would swing. A little piece of white moving around as a distraction...like him choking on a piece of fruitcake during Nick Price's downswing at Wentworth. Apparently, he picked this up from Peter Thomson, the Australian. Of course, I would never do this...but you know I wear white shoes. Something for you to think about on the tee box."

We cackled all the way to the first tee.

The calluses in my brain were starting to thicken. Bondy no longer intimidated me. He amused.

Standing on the first tee, we looked to our right at the cliffs bordering the ocean then to our left at the gorse-framed holes. As he put his tee in the ground, Bondy smirked, "So, young Mr. Reese..." He made a sweeping gesture, pointing out the scenery for dramatic effect: "Until today you have never lost a match in your ancestral homeland."

He then smoked his tee shot up an enormous hill with a small flock of sheep grazing.

Many courses in Wales have animals on them. Lots of animals. At nearby Pennard, wild horses roam freely. Aberdovey has hundreds of cows. Watch your step. Many other courses take the sheep theme seriously. Keeps down the mowing costs.

Bondy's drive barely missed the flock about two hundred yards out. Mine was not so lucky. Bummed me out—not the sheep, it barely noticed. Like making contact with a fluffy pillow. No roll. Long second shot in.

Now to the fourth hole.

Enid Day

TONY

We waited by the fourth green as the two Welshmen played into us. After two quick putts, the elder Welshman called the hole a half. They were low-handicap speedsters. As they looked at number five, terror washed over them. They saw the same slow-moving foursomes we had seen. The second group had already spent twenty minutes impersonating mountain climbers scaling the hillside green.

Making matters worse, I asked, "We've waited here for a while. Would you like to join us?" My accent may have been the last straw. Hearing my voice, visions of five-hour rounds in golf carts circled in their heads.

"That's very kind. Thank you anyway, but we're fine," one of them demurred. "We're in the middle of a match. You two go ahead, but thank you anyway, that's very kind. Cheers." I was still about a twelve handicap, but had a reasonably nice swing, and thanks to Angus' putting drill, putting was becoming a problem of the past.

As the green cleared, I teed my ball and took a few practice swings. Prayed for solid contact. The two gentlemen watched. With a swing to remember, I struck the ball pure with my seven iron. I wanted to hold my pose but thought better of it. Absolutely stiff. The ball hit the green and checked up less than ten feet from the pin. Imitating Angus, I gave a small shrug as if to indicate that I had intended to hit a fade with this wind. Bondy then calmly hit his inside mine.

The older of the two gentlemen spoke first: "Would you mind terribly if we joined you? It doesn't look as if we're going to get through the groups in front of us." I had never played my way into someone's group before. I felt like Angus or Bondy. A golfer's acceptance.

They introduced themselves as Ken and Tony, both playing to mid-single digits. We played for the next four holes before Ken tired of playing hit-and-wait golf. After bidding Ken goodbye, Tony suggested that we skip a few holes, leapfrogging the groups in front of us. Bondy and I had long since given up on our individual match. We played well. We played fast. We hit it off immediately. Post round, we exchanged phone numbers, promising to get together again for more golf.

THE WELSH COURSES

Now late, Bondy and I had to hurry to our hotel to greet the incoming golf group from the States. The next few days, we played several courses. The first day, Pyle & Kenfig, with its great back nine set amongst breathtaking dunes, filled the morning. In the afternoon, we played the beastly Royal Porthcawl in a serious wind. With nearly all holes overlooking the sea, Porthcawl presented a true championship test. Definitely the best course in Wales.

On day two, we played 36 at Pennard, one of the most spectacular, yet quirky, golf courses we had ever been on. Small wires were strung around the green to keep out the wild horses, which ran around as if someone were filming a movie. In the middle of the course, a few of the holes played past a ruined castle. Set out on cliffs, the views on holes sixteen and seventeen made me as excited as a toddler on Christmas morning—I couldn't wait to hit my tee shot. All of us appreciated Pyle & Kenfig, respected and admired Porthcawl, but were smitten with Pennard.

After two days of 36 holes each, half of our group took a day off. Before he left, Bondy waxed romantic about Southerndown. A few of us decided to play there.

We called our new friend Tony.

The others were equally taken in by the cliff-side views, the gorse-bush-lined fairways, and the omnipresent sheep. Following Bondy's cue, we gave no relief for hitting sheep. "Rub of the Green. Play it as it lies unless you are in droppings. Then lift, clean, and place is acceptable. But don't use my towel."

Around the seventh hole, we noticed Tony walking towards us. After introducing himself to the others, he handed us each fifteen pounds, explaining, "I'm terribly sorry I wasn't here when you arrived, but I checked you in. You now get the member's guest rate."

Tony then picked up my small Sunday golf bag and proceeded to caddie for me. Assume, you're a fit 37-year-old. A guy in his mid-60s signs you in as his guest, gives you money, and insists on caddying for you. How do you respond? Just say thanks.

We all enjoyed the round so much more because he was there. Tony took us to lunch. We didn't have to tell the waitress that Americans out-tip the Welsh. She let me handle the bill. It was the least we could do. As we left, Tony said to us, "So, when will we play again?" We knew it would be soon.

A few months later, Tex and I went to meet Bondy in the UK to play golf for the weekend. We planned to play The Berkshire, Rye, and Royal St George's. We ran into Tony at the baggage claim at Heathrow. Small world.

After exchanging pleasantries and introducing him to Tex, I got down to business: "We are playing The Berkshire this afternoon. Bondy is waiting in the car." Our words were more statements than questions.

"Love to play. Let me work out a few details," he answered. This exchange should make it clear why we became such fast friends.

As we walked to the car, Bondy flashed a huge grin and said, "Well, this is one for the memory banks, being joined by the finest player from Wales...after Ian Woosnam...but a wee bit taller." It was a sunny Friday afternoon, and we were on our way to another adventure. Tom, Huck, and two ol' friends were headin' to the river. Aunt Polly couldn't stop us.

Over the next few years, we frequently met Tony. Not big fans of small talk, our calls would go something like this:

"What's your schedule the next few weeks?"

"Budget meetings in Helsinki. I'll be in London after that. We could probably tee off at 6:00 p.m. at Wentworth on Wednesday the 24th."

"See you there."

We didn't need to say more.

He became a regular. On our drive back to the airport after one of our trips, he asked about my Welsh father. I mentioned that my dad would be having prostate surgery soon.

Tony put his hand on my arm and said, "We all have prostate cancer. But most of us die with it, not from it. You know I have prostate cancer too. They don't even treat it in gentlemen of my age because it grows so slowly."

Strangely comforted, I asked, "What are you doing with yours?"

Tony switched topics. "This really was one of the finest courses I've played." Those were among the last words we ever heard him speak.

Tony passed away shortly thereafter.

He left a note with his wife for me to be called after he passed. He never told us he had serious cancer.

Although he was the consummate soft-spoken Welsh gentleman, Tony grabbed life. He never let go till the end.

I'm thankful I hit that good seven iron.

CHAPTER X

~

THE ACCOUNTANT

Our senior management team held working capital meetings in Dublin one year. A great links course at the end of the day relieved the pressure of the morning's finance meetings.

On the first afternoon, we played Portmarnock Golf Club. Our team thrashed Angus & Co. *seven and six.* That evening at dinner, an ebullient Bondy toasted Angus: "For those of you who weren't born before the Great War, we call that score a dog's license. A long time ago, a dog's license cost seven shillings and six pence." Bondy imitated a dog whimpering, setting the tone for the next few days.

On day two, our controller, one of the members of Angus' team, had to bow out: "Would it be possible to replace me this afternoon?" Angus turned to Bondy and said, "Don't worry, I won't use one of the pros at the club. I'll find an accountant or somebody like that."

"Fair enough, but I'll expect you to come up with a pretty spectacular ringer," answered Bondy. "The last time you did this to us, you brought the bandit of Waterville." He was referring to the nine-handicap member who joined us in a downpour and promptly shot a better score than Angus. They crushed us *five and four*. Over a post-round cup of Waterville's famous hot whiskey drink, Bondy groaned, "I may look like I just sailed up the Firth of Clyde in a banana boat, but they do handicaps differently here. Played against the Highwayman of Kerry today."

ROYAL DUBLIN

That afternoon, we drove a few miles down the coast to the Royal Dublin Golf Club (Dollymount). My hero, lawyer-turned-golf-course-architect Harry Colt, built the course, along with Sunningdale New, Muirfield, Royal Portrush, St George's Hill, and part of Pine Valley. Reasonable résumé.

Colt's courses require strategic positioning to score well. The greens are subtle, but an out-of-position shot will have a tough time holding the green or getting close to the pin. Further, they look incredibly natural, as if almost no earth were moved to build them.

Royal Dublin combined many of these elements on a piece of linksland that was not naturally awe-inspiring. Unlike many of the great Irish courses, there are no high dunes or spectacular sea views at Royal Dublin. Of course, this being a links course, smokestacks served as aiming points off in the distance.

THE ACCOUNTANT

As we pulled into the driveway, Angus jumped out of the van, making a beeline for the clubhouse. "I'll check with the Secretary to see if he can score up someone to play on our side. Don't worry, Bondy, it will be an accountant."

Bondy chuckled.

As I walked out of the pro shop and into the club-house, Angus and his new partner were having tea. He was indeed an accountant. A CPA to be exact. But a wee bit better than our 24-handicap controller who had bowed out. This one had a name, a reputation, and a list of honors. Future three-time Major winner and six-time Ryder Cupper. Good-natured, boyish Pádraig Harrington. An excessive ringer, even by Angus' lofty standards.

Upon seeing Pádraig, Bondy exclaimed, "So Angus replaces our controller with Pádraig Harrington. Next thing you know, he'll replace his two Finnish partners with those well-known Finns, Darren Clarkaskangas and Paul McGinleyainen." His hand resting heavily on my shoulder, Bondy continued, "Well, partner, if Angus loses with Pádraig, we'll talk about it until the next Ice Age."

Pádraig gave a look that said, "Game on."

The Teams

Our four-man team was a mixed bag. Bondy and I usually shot within a few strokes of our handicap but rarely made birdies. One look at my set of irons told the story. My sand wedge got a lot more use than any other club in the bag. And not because of how far I drove the ball.

Our partners, Tex and Javier de Moragas, both exhibited a natural flair for the dramatic. Javier was our country manager for Spain. Like Tex, Javier delivered great business results and was an excellent athlete. They called themselves the Conquistadors. And like their namesakes, things could go really well or really badly. There was one other issue. Conquistadors are averse to both the cold and wet weather. The current conditions were 50 degrees and raining sideways.

Facing our team, Angus and Pádraig had Kari and another stoic Finn as partners. The Finns wouldn't notice the cold or the rain, and they got a lot of strokes. But their games didn't hold up well under tough links conditions. As there were eight of us, we wanted to give everyone a chance to play with Pádraig. Pádraig and Angus would play the front nine with the Conquistadors. Then they would play the back nine with Bondy and me.

THE MATCH

After a bit of haggling, Bondy confirmed, "Full stroke differential, and Pádraig is a zero." He then added, "He hits from the furthest back tees...I'll be searching for a tee box at a neighboring golf course if I have to."

The main match:

Pádraig and Angus vs. Bondy and me.

As he put his tee in the ground, Bondy turned to the crowd and said, "Well, Gussie and Pádraig, here's one for the memory banks...likely a historic upset." He then stepped back and leaned against his driver: "Have I mentioned that I have never been beaten by a former Scottish Amateur Champ and a future Ryder Cupper while partnering with a young American farmer?" He stopped talking long enough to hit his low runner down the middle.

As the rest of us teed off, the wind drove the rain sideways into our faces. Umbrellas were useless. To try to keep warm we had wool caps and baggy, stiff rain suits. That would have to suffice.

For the first six holes, Bondy and I made a series of pars and bogeys. Kari and the other Finn played consistently. Consistently badly. The weather didn't bother them, but the course did. Our focus was on the group behind us.

Bondy peered through misty glasses to glimpse our pursuers. "I see two guys walking down the middle of the fairway," Bondy laughed. "Unfortunately, I see a Spaniard with his nose pointed towards the ground like a wet Labrador and a Texan next to him. The Conquistadors must be conquering some small village in the high grass. Not exactly Cortés or Pizarro."

While we switched players after nine, Bondy smiled and casually remarked to Tex and our Spaniard, "The two formidable Finns must be sitting on a pond ice fishing. Haven't written down a score for them in a while."

The Spaniard was too cold to reply. Tex smiled and chimed in, "Harrington made nine straight pars, and I made a birdie on six. Just the highlights, right?"

Prior to teeing off on ten, we compared scorecards for our straight four-ball match against Angus and Pádraig. We were *all square.*

On our approach to ten, Bondy and I missed the green. Pádraig stuck his approach to about fifteen feet. Bondy and I both chipped to within gimme range for scrappy pars. Pádraig missed his birdie by a razor's edge.

This pattern repeated itself for the next four holes. With the rain falling steadily and wind coming hard, his birdie putts weren't falling. At one point, Bondy pointed out, "Harrington reminds you of Nick Faldo making eighteen pars at Muirfield. In this weather. Incredible to watch."

On the fifteenth tee box, Bondy whispered to me, "Keep making those ugly pars of yours. We both get shots here and then again on eighteen."

"Can I assume ugly in Scottish translates to effective and valuable?"

"As your partner, they're a thing of beauty."

The hole played almost straight into the wind. True to form, Pádraig hit another green in regulation, while Bondy and I came up just short. Our balls were less than a foot from each other. Bondy chipped to five feet. I felt confident. Unlike putting, I loved chipping.

I always expected to get it close.

But this time I caught the ball thin. It raced off in the direction of the hole. Glad I was not a pilot landing on an aircraft carrier.

Then golf happened.

The ball hit the flagstick. Popped straight up in the air. Buried in the cup.

Pádraig smiled and shook his head: "Classic birdie."

One up.

FINAL HOLE

Despite Harrington's display of control golf, we were still *one up* as we got to eighteen.

Standing on the tee, Bondy turned to me and said, "You know, this hole is like the one at Royal Liverpool (Hoylake). It's a huge dogleg, and everything to the right of the ditch is OB." Of course, I hit it there. Thanks for mentioning it, Bondy.

Bondy was in the fairway and pulled out his five wood, his standby. He took a short backswing and rifled a bullet at the stick. It landed in front of the green before rolling twenty feet short of the cup. There in net one. On cue, Pádraig hit his shot just inside Bondy's.

I counseled Bondy: "We're one up. You lie net one. If you've got two putts, use 'em."

Bondy nodded then lined up the putt carefully, murmuring, "A few inches outside, but at the end of the day, it's really all about pace." Bondy leaned into his putter with his trademark wide stance and his knees leaning in towards each other. His pre-KJUS rain suit sagged.

Resigned, Pádraig watched from the other side of the green. He'd watched far better golfers than Bondy stalk twenty-footers. But he hadn't seen a better putt. Bondy's ball moved towards the hole, ignoring all impediments, making a rain-muffled sound when it fell in the cup. It never had a chance to miss.

Imitating Hale Irwin at Medinah, Bondy raced around the green looking for someone to high five.

Nobody there.

As he came to me, Bondy said, "Now, there's one for the memory banks. Angus being carried by his partner and losing to an Old Scot and a young kid from Ohio."

Two up.

In my golf library, the framed scorecard rests next to a hat, which bears the writing:

Bondy and Luke,
"Next Time!"
Pádraig Harrington.

CHAPTER XI

~

THE SURPRISE

Working for a multinational corporation, I frequently travelled to far-flung places. My standard rotation took me to Helsinki, London, Barcelona, Paris, Scotland, and Austria. I also spent a fair amount of time in parts of Russia, the Middle East, and North Africa.

Not all places were safe.

When I visited Tel Aviv, bombs went off nearby in the West Bank. Nobody flinched. We kept selling. In Johannesburg, we were told not to fasten seat belts so that carjackers wouldn't shoot us if we reached to unclick them. In Moscow, we encountered a secret service raid at the Kempinski hotel. The good guys—we think—wore black masks. Border control in Tunisia decided that the pictures of Steffi Graff in our tennis catalogue were pornographic. They sat me in an interrogation room for eight hours. I responded by falling asleep.

By far the best: I missed my scheduled flight to Thessaloniki, Greece. It got hijacked and spent the day on the tarmac in Athens. Despondent because his girlfriend had broken up with him, the hijacker first tried to impress her by hijacking a plane then decided to kill himself by swallowing a cross. Neither plan worked.

But of all these places, my wife's biggest fear was visiting Northern Ireland.

In fairness, in the '80s and early '90s, the violence in Northern Ireland had received a lot of press. However, despite my protestations that the violence was confined to certain areas, her fears persisted.

The Course

Even with my marital prohibition on going to Northern Ireland, I pined over Royal County Down (Newcastle). *Classic Golf Links* fueled my longing for the course. Tauntingly, the editors had placed a picture from the fourth tee on the back cover. The Mountains of Mourne and church spires in the background beckoned. The characteristic bunkers, with their long grass whiskers, blended in seamlessly. I could smell the fresh salty air. Feel the crisp breeze. Obsessive personality? Whatever. Time spent looking at the pages passed like seconds.

Enid Day

THE DECISION

My wife's fear of Northern Ireland was eclipsed only by my desire to play there. About three weeks prior to our planned working capital meeting in Dublin, where we would have our epic match against Angus and Pádraig, I got a call from Bondy and Angus.

The call went something like this. "It's Angus and Bondy. We've got a small issue. We mentioned to the buyer from one of our biggest accounts, Grahame Jenkins, that we would be in Dublin for a meeting. He wants to take you to play Royal County Down. With him being from Northern Ireland, we couldn't tell him that you weren't allowed to go there. How should we proceed?"

Synapses firing, I contemplated my answer...for at least a millisecond.

"Awesome. I can't wait."

They finished the call with, "Great. We'll leave early after the Dublin meetings and fly out of Belfast that afternoon."

With a huge pit in my stomach at the prospect of sneaking off to Northern Ireland, I opened my worn copy of *Classic Golf Links* and quickly reviewed the pictures of County Down. Then I read Tom Doak's review in the *Confidential Guide.* 10/10 on the Doak scale, which translates to "Nearly perfect...drop the book and call your travel agent, immediately." Any hesitation vanished. I was over-come with anticipation.

For the next few weeks, I not so subtly tried to break down barriers around going to Northern Ireland. Copies of peace process articles mysteriously showed up around our apartment.

They went unread.

While watching videos one rainy day in Munich with my two young daughters, I had a small brush with danger. Thirteen-month-old Olivia had picked the schedule. Four-year-old Madeline[1] had negotiated on their behalf, and after reaching an agreement we were all quite happy.

First bacon. Then *Barney* and *Irish Links* accompanied by gummy bears and apple juice. Followed by *Arthur*, more *Irish Links*, and *Curious George*, with a side of ice cream and second round of apple juice. During a segment on Royal Portrush, my wife arrived home. The smell of bacon grease hung in the air, and the three of us were lying on the floor in a pile of candy wrappers. The room lacked adult leadership. I braced for "Lucy, you got some 'splainin' to do!" Shockingly, her only comment was "You're not playing Royal Portrush. That's in Northern Ireland."

"Nope."

We three amigos returned to our party.

---

[1] Yes. The editor of this book.

Northern Ireland

Back to our meetings in Dublin. That night, a particularly jocular Bondy bought a round of Guinness in honor of the vanquished Angus and Pádraig.

The next morning, at 0-dark-30, we slipped away from the hotel as quietly as ninjas. Direction: Northern Ireland. Before we pulled away, I reminded Bondy and Angus, "It would be best if my wife does not find out for a while. I'm just glad this junket has a business purpose."

Once the car started rolling, I slept soundly. I think I respond to stress differently from others. According to Angus, the only thrill came when the border guards shined a spotlight on my stiff body. They were about to open my door when I let out a snore. Instead they waved us through.

I woke up, well rested, outside Newcastle and caught my first live glimpse of the Mountains of Mourne and the expansive Irish Sea. Maybe I was in heaven. Bondy's greeting disabused me of that thought: "Hope you slept well. We're a little lost here. We don't have a map."

"If the picture of County Down had a lawyer, it could get a restraining order against me," I yawned. "From the first tee, the sea is on the right, the town is at your back, and the mountains are behind that. Go around the bay. It will be off to the right."

"He's from that well-known links golf area...Ohio," Bondy chuckled. "Let's go his way."

On schedule, we pulled into the driveway.

We changed in the visitors' locker room and hustled to the first tee. "Where's Grahame?" I asked. Bondy answered, "He might be running a little late." As we got to the first tee, Angus took a few practice swings. I looked around for Grahame.

Finally, Angus handed me a card. It read: "Surprise! Belated happy birthday." It was signed by my wife.

I had taken the bait. Like an unsuspecting trout, I had risen to an artfully cast fly. Swallowed the hook.

Angus said, "Happy Birthday. Grahame's not coming. I'll take you two on. One ball against two. Five shots each. Quick round. Got a plane to catch."

Angus then ripped one down the middle on the opening par-five. As the ball was still in flight, he turned and cracked, "No mulligans."

Dunes to my left. Sea to my right. Wind at my back. With the knowledge that I was allowed to be here, I hit my drive past Angus. "Must have hit a sprinkler head, young Mr. Reese," Bondy commented. Angus smiled appreciatively. We all strode purposefully down the fairway with our caddies trailing behind. Nothing could be better.

THE MATCH

The majesty of Royal County Down, coupled with the birthday surprise, rendered me temporarily speechless.

Not an easy task. On the first hole, I floated down the fairway, turning around occasionally to see the barren mountains and the church spires rising out of the city. Looking ahead, I could see the grass-bearded bunkers. Preferring to experience those from afar, I gave my shots a wide berth. After I made an easy par, Angus ran his birdie putt too hard past the hole. Surprisingly, he missed the comeback. Bondy and I were *one up*.

On number four, we climbed up to the tee on the 217-yard par-three. In the words of Bernard Darwin, Royal County Down "is a course of big and glorious carries, nestling greens, entertainingly blinds shots, local knowledge, and beautiful turf...the kind of golf that people play in their most ecstatic dreams." Indeed, it was. Only better.

With a three-club wind in our face, Angus hit a choked-down, low-flying three iron. Like a falcon after a defenseless sparrow, his ball homed in on the flag. Tap in birdie. In response, I pulled out my driver. What a hole. Perfect surprise birthday present. I silently asked the powers above for a hole in one. They thought that might be pushing it.

Back to *all square*.

Coming to the ninth, we shook with excitement. The 486-yard par-four was ranked the best ninth hole in the world. It featured a blind drive into a valley, with the approach playing to a green protected on the right by a massive two-story high dune. Playing straight into an ungiving wind, Angus and I made fives. It was definitely our favorite ninth hole. With a stroke, Bondy and I were back to *one up*.

Bondy had started the day playing poorly and never quite righted the ship. We didn't use his score once all day. Likely, he had spent all his energy beating Angus and Pádraig the day before. Trouble with the driver causes problems at all courses. But the forced carries over the County Down hills magnified these difficulties. Through it all though, he maintained a cheerful façade. Hitting yet another drive into the side of a hill, Bondy looked at me: "I won't allow my bad golf to distract from your great time." I filed his nugget away. Something we can all live by.

On the back nine, Angus made three birdies. I made two. Ecstasy.

Standing on the par-five eighteenth tee, we were *all square*. I smiled as a soft rain began to fall. We were now living the entire County Down experience. Bondy laughed as I pointed out, "You know, Angus, this slight rain brings out my best golf." Shaking his head, Angus could only answer, "Bondy has trained you too well. At this exact moment, I prefer to be playing against a deliberate American, who complains about uneven lies and hates wind and rain." He then hit a cracker down the middle.

On his second shot, Angus went for the green and got stuck at the face of a bunker. His third had to come out sideways. My third ended up fifteen feet from the hole.

Angus chipped to three feet—but above the hole.

Having just three-putted seventeen, I kept my silence. Bondy coached, "Easy here, partner."

Then my caddie, who'd steered me right all day, surprised me by saying, "I don't want a birdie here. This is a dangerous putt if you hit it too hard. Get your par and force your opponent to make his difficult three-footer."

My mind filled with myriad thoughts. Possibly my caddie was gambling with the other caddie. Or maybe Angus had a really tough putt and my caddie just wanted me to make par and ensure the half. As I crouched over the ball, my caddie's comments raced through my mind. He had been right all day.

I stepped back to clear my head. My mind went blank.

I hit my putt. It tracked right to the hole. Dead on line. Then it stopped. Inches short.

Bondy reached out and picked it up, adding, "That's a great par, partner. Now let's see if young Gus can make this sliding five-footer with a double break. That one is called a Diego Maradona or a Danny DeVito...nasty little five-footer."

As Angus lined up his putt, he couldn't suppress his grin. In reality, the putt wasn't more than three feet, but Bondy was on a roll. No stopping him now.

Bondy snickered as Angus lined up his putt for the second time. Bondy put his mitt on my shoulder. Bondy and I smiled at each other and nodded our heads, as I prepared my next move.

Reaching out with my putter, I knocked away Angus' ball and said, "That's good."

All square. We were all winners that day.

Angus quickly stretched his hand out and said, "Cheers. Great half."

What a birthday present...and I got to feel like Jack Nicklaus giving Tony Jacklin a putt.

I ran into the pro shop and bought the official club history of Royal County Down. Bondy wrote on the inside cover, "You played like a god today, partner. I trained you well. I'll take all the credit."

With typical elegance and understatement, Angus wrote, "Nice Day. Nice Course. Nice Half."

I gave my wife an amazing birthday present that year. It didn't compare to Royal County Down.

.

Chapter XII

Petition Denied

After meetings near Edinburgh a few months later, we drove approximately 40 minutes to play the Luffness New Golf Club, another club out of *Classic Golf Links*. The club is located in the tiny town of Gullane, where golf permeates daily life. The town is also home to Gullane One, Two, and Three. Then North Berwick and its famous West Links is another ten miles down the road. In between the two towns sits Muirfield, discreetly hidden away—and cheekily called Gullane Four by some non-member locals. Not too shabby an assortment within a ten-mile radius.

If you're a links golf lover, treat The Old Clubhouse as your temporary *Cheers*. Nobody knows your name. But it won't matter. Bondy mentioned, "You know, my really close friend, Ken Macpherson? His uncle owned this place for years. I used to come here when I would stay at his house in Dunbar. Need to take you there someday."

"Dunbar's a sporty little track," Angus confirmed.

Sitting near the courses at Gullane, The Old Clubhouse faces the town's junior course with its shortened holes and limited hazards. Almost every night, while enjoying a near perfect draught, one can observe mini Bondies practicing bump and runs in matches against junior Angus Moirs.

For years, a sign hung on the course that read, "No Adults Allowed." While watching kids one night, Bondy remarked to our group, "You know, when I grew up, we got a set of clubs instead of a bike." If sitting in an authentic golf bar watching young kids hit knockdowns doesn't make you fall in love with links golf, stay home...or better yet, go to Vegas, turn on loud music, and ride in a cart for five hours.

MUIRFIELD

Like those of the Ayrshire coast of Scotland, the courses in this area vary significantly from one another. Muirfield, home to The Honourable Company of Edinburgh Golfers, dominates the reputation of the area, but not the geography. It is purposefully hidden away. Architecture guru Harry Colt created a straightforward strategic challenge on almost every hole. The routing moves in circles, causing the wind to play from constantly shifting angles. And while Muirfield presents one of the most amazing collections of golf holes anywhere, it lacks classic beauty. Not as scenic as

Royal Dornoch or Turnberry, historic as St Andrews, or majestic as Royal County Down, Muirfield earns its marks the old-fashioned way: eighteen great golf holes. It will seriously test all the ninety-plus shots a ten handicap will hit that day.

Greywalls, the hotel next to the course, offers old-school luxury and a Michelin-starred restaurant. Unlike drinking whisky with Bondy at Machrie, Greywalls is not a place I fantasize about going with him. Would rather order a bottle of pinot noir with a *somewhat* more romantic companion.

Getting a spontaneous tee time at Muirfield is akin to Congress getting along. Theoretically possible. Never seems to happen. For years, an inflexible and imperious club secretary named Paddy Hanmer made the process exceedingly difficult. Dealing with Secretary Hanmer was probably interesting. Once. Muirfield has become appreciably more civil since Secretary Hanmer's retirement.

North Berwick

Muirfield provides the challenge. Gullane offers authentic public golf and The Old Clubhouse. But if I had to play all my rounds at only one course in the area, the West Links at North Berwick would top my list.

The course is nestled snugly between the Firth of Forth and the picturesque town of North Berwick. It overflows with history and ambience. Standing on the course, you can imagine Old and Young Tom Morris coming over from St Andrews to play challenge matches. Bass Rock, a huge volcanic island, sits just off the coast providing a dramatic background for many holes. On the second hole, the beach is in play. A few years before, Bondy made par from the beach with his five wood. Responding appropriately, I three-putted.

On a few holes, an old farmer's stone wall forms an integral part of the strategy, particularly on a hole called Pit. It has a short approach over the wall to a tiny punchbowl green. You have to hit your drive close to the wall to have the right angle to get to the green. Quirky and a blast—especially when you leave Pit *one up*, after Bondy has left his approach shot on the wrong side of the wall.

In addition to its historic value and beauty, North Berwick contributed a great deal to course architecture. North Berwick's Redan—number fifteen—is one of the most copied par-threes in the world. If getting a tee time at Muirfield is passing through purgatory, playing North Berwick must be heaven.

On a previous trip, over a bottle of wine at Greywalls, long-time North Berwick professional David Huish held court. David led The Open after two rounds at Carnoustie the year Watson won it. He explained how the architecture and strategy at North Berwick had evolved over a century ago: "The club would invite several great golfers to play. After multiple rounds, the course stewards would then find the groupings of divots where the players had hit their approach shots to the greens. Assuming that skilled players had figured out the proper angles for approaching greens, they placed a small fence around the divots and allowed sheep to graze there for a while, creating a bunker. Now the good player had to flirt with the bunker or hit from a more difficult angle."

Genius.

Continuing his stories, David added, "When I first joined the Senior Tour, they handed me a scorecard and there were some Xs next to some holes. So, I asked, 'I get strokes?' The answer: 'Nope, those are the locations of the toilets. Welcome to the Senior Tour.'"

We happily bought dinner and wine to keep the storytelling tap primed.

LUFFNESS NEW

The next morning, Bondy, Angus, and I went to play Luffness New Golf Club. David had arranged our tee time well prior. We pulled up to the modest clubhouse, situated just off the main road in Gullane. Straightening his tie, buttoning his coat, and patting down his wind-blown silvery hair, Bondy made himself presentable. I watched as Bondy and Angus disappeared around the clubhouse. We couldn't have chosen two more respectable emissaries.

Meanwhile, I sat in a small, steamed-up rental car. I didn't dare open the door or put down the windows. No phones allowed on property, and I was trying to finish the business calls I needed to make. Thirty minutes later I was at the end of my to-do list, and the car was sweltering—*what was taking them so long?*

I imagined Bondy and Angus had probably accepted an invitation for a cup of tea. Most likely Bondy had made a keen observation about one of the names on a wooden plaque. Almost certainly that would have started Bondy and the old Secretary trading stories. This presumably would all have occurred while they took a long, sweeping tour of the clubhouse. I'd have to settle with buying a club history book. Not to worry. Bondy had a great eye for detail and wasn't shy about sharing; I would get the full story later.

I could not have been more wrong.

Shortly thereafter, a red-faced Bondy bulldozed around the corner of the clubhouse followed by a shocked Angus, shaking his head in disbelief.

This is their story.

THE REQUEST

After patting down his hair and straightening his tie, Bondy led the small, but distinguished, delegation to handle the details of our prearranged tee time. Standing in the 50-degree cold on the wind-exposed side of the club-house, they knocked on the office door. Through a sliver in the blinds, the Secretary, a retired Lt. Colonel, peered out at the two supplicants. Quickly and emphatically, the blinds snapped shut. The Secretary then returned to the pressing business of scanning his morning paper. For the next ten minutes Bondy and Angus patiently stood outside his door. Aware that Luffness New had a reputation of being exclusive, they assumed the Secretary was snubbing them for arriving prior to official opening hours. They were near Muirfield after all.

Angus waited patiently. Bondy began to percolate.

Having firmly established who was in charge, the Secretary opened his door slightly and asked what business they might have with Luffness New Golf Club. Bondy responded, "Good morning, sir, we have a tee time under the name of Moir or Bond." The Secretary took the statement dubiously, responding, "I see. Let me check my book." Bondy might as well have been Oliver Twist asking for more porridge.

The Secretary did not invite them in from the cold. The Secretary did, however, conduct a slow and dutiful review of the day's groups, checking the list a few times before responding, "No, gentlemen, I do not find any tee time for today under the name Bond or Moir. I'm afraid there must be a mistake. Maybe you wish to play the public course at Gullane." Although the Secretary's words made Bondy redden, a diplomatic Angus gently suggested that the reservation might be found under the names David or Martyn Huish (David's son).

In response to Angus, the Secretary turned away, clearly stating, "Gentlemen, I'll check my book again and get back to you." He closed the door to his office once more. Moving at a glacial pace, he picked up the book and gave it another thorough review. He then resumed reading his newspaper. Remaining in the frigid wind, Angus and Bondy could only watch. The Secretary had something they wanted. He was going to make them wait.

Five minutes later, he picked up his phone and made a few phone calls. As the Secretary hung up the phone, he consulted his book once again, scanning the day's calendar. He opened the door for Angus and Bondy but blocked them from entering by standing directly in their paths.

He scanned his book for a third time, "No entries for Bond. No entries for Moir. No entries for Huish. No entries for David Huish. No entries for Martyn Huish either." And that was the end of the matter. Everything was above board, but somebody had forgotten to write it down in the Secretary's book.

Angus and his patient diplomacy could get them no further; Bondy would take over matters from here. With his eyes glowering, Bondy forced a smile. He suggested the Secretary call David Huish at North Berwick and clear up this minor inconvenience. Bondy's smile barely hid his contempt.

With the latest request from Bondy, the now put-out Secretary decided to make things personal. He opened his book for Bondy and Angus to examine. The only writing on the page was the date. Nothing else. No tee times for the entire day. The Secretary had been pretending to examine an empty page. Bondy boiled.

The *coup de grâce* was about to come. "My good man," he said, coldly staring at Bondy. "As you can very well see, you are not on the list for today. You are not on the list for tomorrow. You were not on the list for yesterday. It is a *never, never. Never happened. Never will.*" Then pointing his finger at Bondy's chest, he added, "*You do not exist.* Goodbye." He closed the door.

God had spoken.

A speechless Bondy and an amazed and embarrassed Angus stood in front of the clubhouse door for a moment in complete shock. They returned to the car and told me the story. After the initial surprise, I burst out laughing. Angus joined in.

But not Bondy.

The belittling treatment by the Secretary provided a much greater memory than a single round of golf. Angus retold all aspects of the story several times. But Bondy could barely talk.

Three years later, after the imperious Secretary retired, a few of us returned to Luffness New. Apparently, we were not alone in having been mistreated by him. Several members and the new Secretary apologized, and our story brought more than a few smiles and offers of free rounds of drinks. Because of his son's graduation, Bondy was unable to join us. We sent him the club history book.

There was no mention of Bondy.

He did not exist.

CHAPTER XIII

~~~

THE IRISH BONDY

In the spring of 1999, Angus asked me to handle a meeting with a potential clothing licensee. I had already agreed, when Angus added, "It's in Dublin, and he wants to take you to play Portmarnock."

I could hear Bondy in the background: "Angus got dog-licensed there. He doesn't want to go back...even adding Pádraig for the meeting wouldn't help."

When's my flight?

Having been to Ireland several times in the intervening years, I now hold a few truths to be absolute. The links courses match those of Scotland. At times, the rough is too high—can't control the rain. The Celtic Tiger economy has vastly improved Irish food. Irish roads are narrow. The pubs are inviting. The people have a lot to say. As Bondy advised, "Take yer time in Ireland. It's not Vladivostok."

ALAN SWAN

As I arrived at the offices near the airport, the clothing company president, Alan Swan, warmly greeted me. In a land where highly articulate people abound, Alan excelled. He inhaled air and exhaled well-formed sentences. He led us on a tour of the facility, talking as if he were a mythical character in an Irish legend. His lyrical accent swayed to a rhythm and speed of its own, propelled by an internal gyroscope. I listened, spellbound, for the better part of twenty minutes. I had little to add.

God balanced Alan's abundant charm with his lack of vertical presence. But despite a short swing arc, Alan generated a ton of club head speed and pounded the ball. For many years long-hitting Greg Norman's charisma drove the Tour. Like Norman, Alan wore his hair in a cool, longish look that aptly suited his debonair, cultured European image. As is expected of a clothing company president, Alan's sartorial choices were impeccable. Alan personified the Celtic Tiger.

Richard Webster, Alan's good friend, noted his similarities to Greg Norman, with one chief exception. His height. Webster nicknamed Alan the "Great White Prawn." With the ascent of a certain Eldrick Woods, Alan's nickname morphed into "Tiger Prawn."

After our meetings, Alan took me, along with his quiet UK rep, to play Portmarnock. During the ride to the club, Alan spewed the history of Irish civilization. It went something like this: "We Irish have been around for a long time—mostly started with the Celts a few thousand years ago—then the Vikings—then Saint Patrick made us Catholics—then some monks on a Scottish island made *The Book of Kells*, one of the wonders of the world at the time."

He answered a phone call. "Yes—reservations at Aqua at eight for three. Thank you—see you then."

Without hesitation, he jumped back to the history lesson: "Where was I? We're a mixture of a lot of things, most of them forced on us. First the Vikings came and kicked the shite out of us. Then the English decided they had been missing out on a lot of fun over here—they got in on the action. Admittedly, they built nice buildings in Dublin, but they didn't let us eat much. A bunch of us died—a bunch of us went to America. The rest of us stayed at home and developed a genuine fondness for sad music, accompanied by whiskey or pints of the black stuff."

He took two additional phone calls during the trip—all in a twenty-minute car ride.

PORTMARNOCK

We pulled up to the elegant, red-tiled clubhouse sitting on the water. The views over the fishing village of Howth would not be out of place in Marin County: framed by hills with sailboat-filled harbors and marine fog resting over the ocean.

We unpacked our gear and made our way to the locker room with its beautiful, old, green lockers. The temperature was in the mid-50s with a mild wind. Pretty tame conditions for links golf. In the event of more serious weather, I had a wool hat and a crinkly, wind jacket.

The holes at Portmarnock are straight-forward, but their direction and length vary constantly, requiring every club in the bag. It is frequently referred to as the fairest of the championship links. Similar to Carnoustie and Muirfield—just a bit more picturesque. The par-threes are among the finest in golf.

Portmarnock's number fifteen and Shinnecock's number eleven share the moniker "shortest par-five in the world." The fifteenth hole calls for a long iron to a small, isolated green. The beach runs the length of the hole on the right. Behind the green to the left, sits a huge hill that collects any balls that may have been pulled or aimed away from the ocean. Deep pot bunkers snare even slightly wayward shots.

We quickly made our way to the first tee, adjacent to an estuary. Don't miss right. In an act of generosity, Alan gave me his long-time caddie. They had started together ten years before when the softhearted Alan allowed a tiny lad ("No bigger than a golf bag") to pull a cart for him.

On that day, Caddie Master Brendan Savage told Alan he only had a caddie with no experience—first time out. Walking down the fairway on the opening hole, Alan noticed the eleven-year-old stepping off a distance. "That will be 147 to the middle, with 128 to cover the front bunker, and 161 to the back edge," said the first timer in a voice that hadn't yet changed.

Shocked, Alan looked at his pint-sized caddie: "Are you a golfer?"

Enid Day

"No. I don't play golf," the little caddie responded. "But I thought I might get a job today, so I came here at 6:00 a.m. and stepped off the course. I wrote it all down in this book. My name is Aidan Doyle, and I'm your new caddie."

The two of them played together for fifteen years without fail. Aidan never caddied a single round for anyone else—except this one round for me. Surpassing his rank as an excellent caddie, Dr Aidan Doyle, PhD, became one of Ireland's leading scientists in optical physics. He now runs the European Patent Office for medical equipment.

WEBSTER'S BUNKER

On the first tee, Alan cranked his drive up the middle and swaggered. I took about three practice swings and listened as my caddie told me to avoid the bunkers on the left and the water on the right. No advanced degree in physics required there.

He didn't plan on my low grounder up the right side, which found a deep pot bunker about two hundred yards from the tee. Stepping off the tee, Alan remarked, "Oh, feck, that one could be trouble." Feck is the Irish "gentle" form of its American cousin. According to Alan, it can be used in polite company. "I hope you didn't go into Webster's bunker. A problem in that one I'm afraid," he continued.

Sure enough, my ball was right in the middle.

Of course, Alan had a story about everything, even the bunker. Yes, the bunker. I wondered what the etiquette was. Should I play the shot, then listen to the story?

Listen to the story, then play the shot? Do both at once? While I frequently talk during my own swing, this was new.

Over the years, I've learned golf in Ireland is played at a considerably slower pace than in Scotland. In Scotland, a four ball gets around in about three hours. The Irish also play ready golf. However, they add 45 minutes of storytelling and banter per round.

"You should probably take your medicine and come out sideways, then you'll have—" Alan suggested as my ball floated past him on to the fairway.

Without missing a beat, he continued, "Now, what is the significance of the name Webster, you ask?" Alan was willing to share all that he knew...and a bit more.

"Longtime Portmarnock member Frank Webster, who won the North of Ireland Championship in the '40s and who played for the Irish International team, had many encounters with that bunker over the years. As an elder gentleman, Mr. Webster had trouble getting out of the steep bunker. He could hit his ball out, but his playing partners would have to hold a club for him to pull himself out. He complained often of this bunker to the committee."

After years of hearing Mr. Webster's complaints, the committee decided to install steps in the bunker for the elder members. On the dedication, Mr. Webster said, "When I was a young man, I hit the ball so far, I never knew the bunker was here. As I got older, I hit into it all the time. Then I'd get stuck in it. Now that I'm really old, you've finally put steps in here to help me. For that I thank you. Unfortunately, your timing is amiss. I can't hit my drive far enough to get into it anymore."

As we putted out on the first hole—yes, we were still on the first hole—Alan mentioned, "Now, Frank Webster is the father of two of my best friends, Peter and Richard Webster. Lovely fellows. And fine golfers. We'll have to have a game with them next time you're back." We did.

The Scenery

To Alan's melodic tune, I was playing the golf of my life.

As we approached the seventh hole, Alan explained, "This is the only par-tree"—Dublin accent— "on the front nine. But it's a beauty. Not too long, but lots of trouble if you miss." For the 100 yards in front of the tee, tall grass and gorse bushes grow wildly, and the green sits amongst low dunes. Inspired by the beauty of the scene, I hit a seven iron to about twenty feet—just on the wrong side of a small mound. Again, my leprechaun cheerleader made me feel great: "Oh, that's lovely. But it will take some fine putting to get your par." As my ball settled within an inch of the cup, one of the caddies exclaimed, "Great putt."

"That's not a great putt," Alan interjected. "I'm sorry, gentlemen, but that's a *very good* putt. As Frank Webster would say, 'A great putt always makes a sound.'"

Coming down nine, Alan pointed out the large ship's mast near the clubhouse. "I'm not positive, but I'm relatively certain that the ship's mast was used as a communication device in the old days. You see, Portmarnock is on linksland separated from *terra firma* by a shallow estuary. A boat or a high-wheeled carriage ferried golfers back and forth to the club. The club would raise a certain flag to indicate that a member wished to be picked up. I'm pretty sure that's true. But I'll have to check on that to make sure."

Alan was an encyclopedia on speed.

The Shot

As we came off eleven, Alan began to tell us about the next hole: "This par-tree coming up is one of my favorites—although it's the fifteenth, along the water, that's the famous one."

Famous or not, I loved number twelve. Huge dunes covered in tall grass that swayed in the breeze rose up behind the elevated green, its massive false front blending into a really mean bunker. Plenty of opportunities for a four-putt. You need an advanced degree in applied mathematics to have even a chance of figuring out the angles.

My appreciation for the hole was not matched by my shot making.

After I'd hit, our playing partner, who had said about ten words up to that point, asked Alan how much wind he thought there was. Not capable of giving a short answer such as, "It's a two-club wind," Alan began, "Well, it depends on what kind of shot you intend to hit..."

As Alan continued explaining the different nuances of the options available, our playing partner calmly stepped up and smoothed his mid-iron. It never left the stick. Normally the kiss of death, Alan began to comment, "That one's going to be close. Oh, it's more than close. Feck, that's going to cost you a few pints of Guinness."

Hole in one.

Alan and I jumped up and down, celebrating like World Cup soccer players. On the neighboring eleventh green two Irish golfers whooped it up. Our partner gave a slight upturned smile and said, "That's nice." I'm not sure if his restraint came naturally or after reflecting on how much this would cost him. Luckily for him, it was a quiet weekday.

That night over dinner, I invited Alan to join our upcoming trip at Royal Dornoch. He looked at his schedule. I had given him four days' notice. "Let me see. I'm sort of busy on that Monday, but if I could move my Friday meeting a few hours earlier, I could just manage to make it." He did.

Four days later, he was sitting in front of a fire at the Glenmorangie Highland Home battling for airtime with Bondy.

According to Irish legend, the Giant's Causeway was created when the Irish giant Finn McCool took on a challenge from the larger, stronger Scottish giant named Benandonner.

With Bondy and Alan Swan, our golf group now had two giant storytellers.

Chapter XIV

If They'd Have Us

How had we ended up at Dornoch? It had started on a damp and chilly night that February. In between bites of pepper shrimp and moo shoo pork, Bondy, Angus, and I discussed—what else?—golf courses.

"What five clubs would you join, assuming they would have you?" Angus asked.

We all scribbled our lists on torn pieces of paper tablecloth. I had to wipe some spilled soy sauce off mine.

Angus	Bondy	Luke
PV	Cuddington	Sunningdale
Shinny	Walton Heath	Portmarnock/County Down
R&A	St George's Hill	Dornoch
RD	Western Gailes	Royal Melbourne/Paraparaumu
Sunningdale	Quinta do Lago	Sand Hills/Cypress

"Solid list, Gus," I added. "No courses outside the world top 30. Don't kid yourself—I'm available for any of those member-guests."

Bondy then gave reasons for his courses. Of course, he digressed. He told stories of James Braid, Mr. Harry Busson, Ken Macpherson, Winston Churchill, Max Faulkner, and Big Brian Barnes.

Six or seven shared plates had come and gone.

"Luker, love our team choices of RD and especially Sunningdale. Didn't you beat Bondy there?"

On cue, Bondy responded, "Don't remember it... but if I did...shouldn't have let you stop at the halfway house and eat your favorite sausage sandwiches. As we all know, a hungry Luke would not have chipped to six inches on the last hole. Then you would have missed the putt and sat under that beautiful oak tree guarding eighteen and cried."

"So, I go for the top courses in the world. Bondy goes local. Luke picks great courses where he can eat," Angus chuckled.

While I ordered more pepper shrimp, Bondy asked, "Where would you take a close friend before the millennium ends?"

Without hesitation, Angus and I said, "Dornoch."

"Never played that one. Sounds like we know where we're going for our last golf trip of the millennium."

"Bondy, we said *close friend*. What makes you think you're invited?"

The pepper shrimp arrived. We began making our plans on a napkin. Royal Dornoch and Cruden Bay would bookend the trip. Because Angus was from Cruden Bay, we would make this a family trip.

Enid Day

Chapter XV

A Fabulous Finish

For our golf trip to end the millennium, we had an unwieldy group of sixteen. Our usually budget-minded approach worked well with a small group of experienced, low-maintenance links golf veterans. But this trip, like most family vacations, would require the patience of a cruise director and the logistical prowess of a D-Day supply officer. Because we viewed ourselves as locals in matters involving UK golf, we did not hire a travel agency. Do *not* follow our example! Far too much hassle.

We tried to keep it simple. Set the time and date. Three rounds at Royal Dornoch. A round each at Brora and Lossiemouth. Then three rounds at Cruden Bay. We didn't care how everyone got there, what they wore, or how they got home. Don't ask, don't tell. Show up on time and *bring cash to pay the caddies!*

The Accommodations

In choosing accommodations, Angus and I walked the line between picking a pricey retreat or a cheap B&B. Despite having Scottish and Welsh fathers, we erred on the expensive side. After all, it was the end of a millennium. In a nice role reversal, sons paid for fathers and hid the bill from them.

On the appointed day, I finished with my meetings at our factory in Irvine. As I got in the car, I called Angus. No answer. I tried Bondy.

"Driving up here was easy," Bondy said. "It's afternoon, I kept the sun on my left, and I drove till I had to use the restroom. I then kept driving about the same distance."

He laughed at his joke till he had to put the phone down.

"When you get to Inverness, follow signs to towns that end in 'bo.' They were all Viking towns up there...remind me to tell you about that one...cross two bridges...but not a third...keep heading north. Now, after the second bridge, every time you have a choice, take the smaller of the two roads and turn away from the sun."

"Is this how they give directions in the Merchant Navy?" I queried. "Do you think the rental car comes with a compass and a sextant?"

I started driving. I always manage to get places.

Bondy's instructions actually worked. I only had to call the hotel once for additional directions. A bag of cookies after I left Glasgow, I found myself on a very small one-car-width road. Sandwiched between hedgerows, I remembered Bondy's advice: "Keep it in the fairway."

I turned into a small crushed stone driveway of an elegant, white manor house, with its crisp grounds stretching for miles. Welcome to The Glenmorangie Highland Home at Cadboll. We had decided on renting the distillery's private house for three days.

Promising from the outside. Better on the inside.

The smell of a peat fire in the comfortable whisky tasting room created the backdrop for the lilting Irish accent of Alan Swan, spinning yarn after yarn. Of course, he was frequently interrupted by snappy rejoinders from Bondy. To keep the conversation fluid, they tested the distillery's various products at the open bar.

THE COURSE

The next morning, we drove twenty minutes north to Dornoch passing the majestic Skibo Castle on the way.

The sight of the castle reminded Bondy to tell me about the Vikings: "So, young Mr. Reese, as I mentioned yesterday...Viking towns all ended in 'bo.' I think 'bo' means village or hamlet in Norwegian...In a battle near Dornoch, the Scottish chieftain grabbed a severed horse leg and killed the invading Viking ruler with it. As fate would have it, he swung the horse leg around while celebrating and cut himself...died a few days later..."

I looked at Bondy in wonderment: "Did you make this shit up?"

"So, remember, young Mr. Reese, if we are all square...I'll grab anything available on eighteen to beat you...but I won't swing it around and get tetanus and die. I'll make you buy me a ham and cheese toastie first...and maybe a wee dram of Glenmorangie malt."

He gave a wry smile, adding, "But this trip, we'll be partners against Angus. So keep hitting those chips close."

As we got to town, Bondy and I exchanged glances of pure joy. The huge cathedral towers over the tiny town of Dornoch. There are a few rows of grey-roofed limestone houses. The smell of wood fires seeps out of chimney stacks. Not much traffic. Google hadn't yet caught on, but if it had, under "charming small Scottish golf town," Dornoch would've popped up first.

With huge smiles, we pulled up to the hallowed ground that shaped Donald Ross.

Royal Dornoch.

At the first tee, Bondy addressed our small army of sixteen golfers plus caddies that had gathered: "Here's one for the memory banks. We Scots repelled the Vikings here...we'll do the same to Angus and his merry band..."

Then he piped one down the middle.

Royal Dornoch has both brains and beauty. It lies in a valley between an immense wall of gorse and the sea. The fairways are quite generous but can lull you into a false sense of security. Being on the wrong side of the fairway makes it difficult to hit and hold the greens. And whatever you do, don't miss the greens. They are perched in the air. Surrounded by rock hard turf. Not great for chipping. An up and down happens only slightly more often than the Cubs have won the World Series.

Standing on the third tee, Bondy pulled out his driver, looked over at us, and proclaimed, "This view ranks right up there with Royal County Down and Turnberry. Glad I'm seeing it with you two before another thousand years passes."

ANGUS' CADDIE

A guardian angel named Stuart Shaw guided Angus. Approaching the third green, Angus turned to his ramshackle caddie, who was wearing worn out work boots, and asked, "So, uh, do you play?" Angus' caddie answered, "Yeah, I like to play."

Reluctantly, Stuart admitted that his name was etched on 80-some-odd trophies, including the Carnegie Shield, one of the oldest trophies in golf. It suddenly became very clear why every read had been perfect.

Lying down on his belly to survey one of Angus' twenty-foot putts, Stuart pronounced, "The grain moves it right, the overall gravity moves it left, the individual slope in the beginning moves it a bit right, but at the end, the small slope moves it slightly left. Past the hole, it runs away. Left edge. Assuming you die it in the hole."

Angus looked at him for final confirmation.

The now standing Stuart said, "Yes, I like left edge, with the final rotation just barely dropping the ball in the cup."

Angus' ball elegantly moved off his putter face and slowly twisted and turned towards the left edge of the hole. Then, as directed by the two maestros, on its final rotation the ball dropped in.

Walking up to the next tee, I asked Stuart about his penchant for slow-paced putts. "When you play as many rounds as I do on a course like Royal Dornoch, you learn that par is a very good score," he answered. "You don't want a lot of four-footers coming back. That could ruin your appetite..."

"...Or make you thirsty," Bondy smirked.

THE MATCHES

With sixteen golfers, we played our usual match but used the top four scores of our group against the top four of their group. We had to assimilate eight new golfers into our teams and try to make it fair. As neither Bondy nor I had seen many of the new golfers play, we relied on the advice of Angus.

A foolish mistake.

They killed us.

After each of the first two rounds at Dornoch, Angus stretched out the announcing of the scoring, but the matches were over by the fourteenth hole. Bondy did not enjoy having Angus smile so much.

ADDRESSING THE HAGGIS

That night, Bondy and I drove back to the Glenmorangie House needing serious comfort. We found it at the open bar. Alan Swan sat by the fireplace telling stories to anyone who would listen. As reliable as an old dog, Bondy added witty details every few sentences. We had our own private House of Commons debating duel, although it was not quite to the level of one of my favorites: "Sir, I do not know whether you will die on the gallows or of the pox." The response: "That depends, my lord, whether I embrace your lordship's principles or your mistress."

As we sat for dinner in the formal dining room, the haunting sound of bagpipes echoed in the distance. Soon, a small procession entered our dining room to present the haggis, a sheep's stomach filled with internal organs and oatmeal. If you haven't been told what it is, it tastes great. But don't trust me—I'm always hungry.

"Haggis is a collection of unmentionable internal ingredients that Scottish cooks—we didn't call them chefs back then—could afford to mix together," said Bondy. "With a bit of single malt, it tastes pretty good."

Prior to the serving of the haggis, Scots recite the very popular poem by Robert Burns called "Address to a Haggis." Fifteen of us unanimously voted to see the Haggis addressed by our beloved elder Scotsman. Bondy happily obliged.

In the poem, the Scottish chieftain pulls out his dagger and brings it aggressively down on the haggis, "warm-reekin', rich!" The hotel staff loved watching Bondy's hammed-up rendition. That was, until he brought the knife down forcefully, smashing the porcelain plate underneath. Angus scooped up the largest piece of the formerly fine china. For quite a while it sat as a trophy in Bondy's office.

The Final Round At Dornoch

For the final round at Dornoch, I paired myself with my dad. He played much better golf than his 26-handicap would indicate. He was streaky and determined. With his stiff swing, Dad hit the ball straight and got surprising distance. Unfortunately, he was one of the worst putters on the planet. It must be genetic.

There was nothing particularly wrong with his stroke. It was his pessimistic attitude.

As a lawyer for 50 years, he had trained himself to look for the downside of any situation. On most putts, Dad moved to swipe the ball back as it left the putter face. He didn't think he'd miss. He knew it.

The Finish

I have always admired friends who put up a bench near a favorite tee box in honor of a departed golfer. If I could have a bench placed for me anywhere in the world, it would be high on the hill on the approach to the seventeenth at Royal Dornoch. It's my favorite view on a links course. That sentiment has only recently been matched by the view of number seventeen at Tara Iti in New Zealand. The 410-yard hole, called Valley, has a huge downslope 200 yards from the tee. Reach it and your ball gets another 50 yards of distance.

However, that extra distance comes at an expense. From the valley below, the second shot must then be played back uphill, over three intimidating bunkers to a punch bowl green. From the tee box, the golfer must decide between two distinct paths. Lay up and have a long, downhill approach shot over a wasteland of gorse. Or hit a regular

Enid Day

drive, with a short, blind uphill approach over bunkers deep enough to hold a 1960s-era Midwestern family plus the fake-wood-veneered station wagon.

On the tee shot, Dad and I went opposite ways: his to the top of the ledge, mine over the hill and down into the valley. Dad hit first—a screamer of a three wood at the green. Because I was down in the valley, I had no idea where it wound up. My knock-down eight iron into the wind looked pretty good. With a huge punchbowl green, it was hard to tell.

As Dad and I walked up the hill towards the green, I told him this was my favorite hole. I patted him on the back; he put his hand on the back of my neck, the way he had before Little League Baseball games. I swallowed my emotions and tried to focus on the match. "Look, Dad," I urged. "We need a par on this hole. Focus on a smooth putt. Don't worry about trying to make birdie. Just get it close because you get two strokes and I get one. This is going to matter. A par will be great."

As we walked over the ridge past the deep bunkers, the green came in sight. There sat two balls one inch apart, not more than five feet from the cup. One was my brand-new ball, and the other was my Dad's scuffed-up X-out.

Dad went first to show me the line, not to make his own putt. Dad got two strokes here. A par would give him a net eagle. With no bad thoughts, because he wasn't trying to make the putt, he putted as smoothly as my athletically gifted mom. Back of the cup. Net hole in one. Not bad.

Now it was my turn. I made contact. The ball dived into the hole, hitting the back of the cup, before making a gratifying plunk as it settled into that blissful darkness.

Two birdies. My dad's and mine. On my favorite hole. Followed by the golfer's hug of a lifetime: net two for me and a net hole in one for dad. We hoped these would help us in our match that we would be tallying up that night at dinner.

We both made long putts on eighteen coming home. Thank you, Dornoch.

Chapter XVI

~

The Playoff

After our final round at Dornoch, we scattered in the general direction of Cruden Bay. The group left behind a trail of evidence: a seven iron, a rain jacket, a wedge, two pairs of wet golf shoes, and three eighteen-ball packs of X-outs. The visitors' locker room looked like one of those tragic, trash-strewn pictures of an Everest base camp. Bondy, Angus, and I gathered the random items.

Before departing, the three of us ate lunch at the Dornoch clubhouse. Continuing our conversation from months before, Angus said, "No doubt about it, Dornoch would be one of my fantasy club memberships."

"I have to say, it's one of my favorites too...the course is matched by the friendliness of the people," Bondy added. "You two join. I'll play as your guest. I might even buy lunch."

We weren't sure how the matches had turned out because we were missing the scorecards from one of the groups.

Opposing captains Angus and Bondy would announce the results that night in the small town of Lossiemouth, halfway between Dornoch and Cruden Bay. Knowing that most of our team had played poorly, we feared another whitewash. "Sorry, partner," Bondy stressed. "Couldn't get it going on the front...came home all right, though." Same sentiments for me.

In Cruden Bay we had been forced to book two hotels. One hotel was decidedly superior to the other. Feeling confident, Angus suggested at lunch that the winning team of that day's Dornoch match stay in the better of the two hotels at Cruden Bay. Reluctantly, Bondy accepted the challenge. The normally reserved Angus was no longer so understated.

Pulling into the town of Lossiemouth on the north coast of Scotland, we found our hotel on the main road right across from the Moray Golf Club. We looked over the railing down onto the course. The road and clubhouse created a natural amphitheater for the first and eighteenth holes. Number eighteen played to an uphill green set just below the clubhouse and only a few yards from the public sidewalk that ran along the right side of the hole. Bondy got out of the car, looked at the windswept landscape, and commented, "Reminds me of St Andrews.

"Speaking of St Andrews, we had a worker from our factory who qualified for The Open there one year.

Can't remember his name...it would have been 1964 or so...anyway...our frugal factory manager made a big deal out of regripping this guy's clubs for him...this was the same factory manager who docked my pay for dropping a wedge and scratching it..."

"Don't hold a grudge for more than 35 years, do we, Bondy?" Angus commented.

"I'm with you, Bondy," I added. "Why let this guy's bad act be diminished by the mere passage of time?"

"We'll make a Scot of you yet," Angus laughed.

"His golf game is there, and he sure plays fast, but we need to work on the Ohio accent," Bondy offered.

Bondy then continued, "So, as I was saying...this guy from the factory...they gave him a staff bag...not sure he even had a caddie. Anyway, so a few of us managed to sneak a dozen new golf balls out of the sales display room... this was back when golf balls came individually wrapped in paper like chocolates. So, here is this guy...can't remember his name..."

"Jimmy something?" Angus chimed in.

Bondy smiled and continued, "So, here is this guy at The Open standing on the first tee at St Andrews. Everybody is watching...including his mother...and he goes to unwrap one of his new balls. He is so nervous he drops the ball into the trash can...now he doesn't make much money...he's not going to lose that ball. So, he dives headfirst right into the trash can on the first tee. Of course, that is right when they announce his name...I think he made a six on the first hole. Probably working at the paper mill in Troon now."

READING THE SCORE

For dinner, each team sat at its own table. Angus and Bondy informed both tables that the winning team would stay at the better of the two hotels that night. The other team high-fived. Our team looked down in resignation. "The beatings will continue until morale improves," Bondy chimed in.

Disappointed with his play, Bondy asked me to read the scores. Bondy *never* willingly handed over the microphone. A quick glance of our scorecard explained why.

As Angus announced his team's score on number five, I preferred to answer, *"Five down."* Angus' team whooped it up. A couple of regulars, who looked like they could have been Bondy's distant cousins, took notice. Bondy pleaded for a quick end to this public execution.

Our team managed two natural pars and two net pars on number six, the spectacular par-three dug into the side of the hill. Miss left and find gorse bushes or a pot bunker. Miss right for a lie ten feet below the green. Our score of twelve—even par—would likely earn a half. Angus paused for effect: "Nine."

An incredulous Bondy fell back in his chair. "What? Three birdies and a par. Did you play from the forward tees?" *Six down* after six.

One of the bar patrons yelled over to us, "Who set up the teams?"

Bondy pointed. Angus shrugged.

On number nine, a short downwind par-five, our team's scores started to improve. Three birdies. It didn't matter. Angus still won the hole. We felt like Butch Cassidy and the Sundance Kid being followed by the best trackers in the world. "Who are these guys?" *Eight down* at the turn.

Somebody on our team said, "Inconceivable." Stealing a line from *The Princess Bride*, I said, "You keep using that word. I do not think it means what you think it means."

As we ate, Bondy asked for handicap certificates of the opposing team. Something was wrong. Eight whining golfers and two pub dwellers agreed.

None of us had ever heard of being *eight down* at the turn. Stretching their pleasure, Angus and his group ordered another pint before resuming. Ten plays downwind most of the time with huge bunkers along the entire front. Avoid those and you only have to worry about a big fall off on the other three sides. No place to miss. Surprisingly, four of our team parred it, eliciting the most magical phrase we'd heard all night: "Nice hole." Only *seven down.*

We won the next few holes as well. Our table sprang to life. A re-energized Bondy grinned, "Not a bad match to halve, aye, Angus?" Bondy's pub friends agreed. Angus grew quiet. Bondy took the card back. He would captain our ship again.

Number fourteen, called Foxy, is a double dogleg with no bunkers. The most famous hole at Dornoch. All of us but Angus got strokes. Bondy and I had made long putts for pars. *Three down.* Four to go. Angus shook his head. The pub regulars turned their stools and hung on every word. Teasing them, Bondy put the card back in his pocket while we ate sticky toffee pudding for dessert. I silently prayed, "Please, let there be enough time to use Dad's net hole in one on seventeen."

Bondy looked at our card and promised a round of drinks for the regulars if we won. A small cheer went up for the self-appointed Walter Hagen. Angus and his team suddenly felt alone.

We won fifteen. *Two down.*

We won sixteen. *One down.*

We came to the seventeenth hole. Angus confidently read his team's score. "Twelve." Four net birdies. Surely a winner.

Bondy paused, then feigning difficulty reading the card. He asked one of the pub regulars for some help. "That would be a *fookin'* ten." Six strokes better than par.

All square.

Angus required an explanation. He got it. Slightly hard of hearing, my dad just winked at me. Scots don't high five. But the prospect of a free pint made them try.

On eighteen, Angus and Bondy agreed that they would announce their score at the exact same time. Not trusting Bondy, Angus made me hold the card. They hesitated. Both of them pump faked. Then, they blurted out, "Thirteen." *ALL SQUARE.* The regulars were crushed.

Bondy remembered his faithful fans and put two "tenners" on the bar. His small, but motivated, fan club drank to his health.

THE PLAYOFF

With only thirty minutes of daylight left, Angus crossed the street to find the Secretary of the Moray Golf Club to arrange a two-hole sudden death playoff. Agreeing that no strokes ought to come into play, we chose two players from each team. Bondy led ours and Mark Harris led theirs.

Bondy liked our chances.

The bar crowd cheered our choice of Bondy and a good athlete from Atlanta. Facing them would be Mark

Harris and a near-sighted guy from Tampa. Darkness would surely not be an issue for him.

"I'll have young Mr. Reese as my looper!" Bondy then declared. "Let's hope he doesn't move as he holds the flag. A little bit jumpy, but he certainly knows how to count."

The small ragtag army of pub dwellers stumbled their way across the street to the first tee to watch the action. Understanding that the letter of the law—and various factual interpretations—might come into play, we gave jurisdiction over the playoff to my dad's best friend, the Honorable Robert M. Duncan, a retired Federal District Court Judge. Justice would be meted out swiftly and surely, but above all, with Bondy-like humor.

Bondy stuck his tee in the ground, musing, "Here's one for the memory banks." Then taking a practice swing, he looked around at the crowd, adding, "Never played late at night with a group of fans and hecklers and a young kid from Ohio on my bag."

All four players found the fairway on their drives, leaving anywhere from 70 to 120 yards on their approaches. Mark pulled out his three wood and aimed at the seventeenth green, 50 yards off-line. I tugged on Bondy's jacket. He gave me a sly grin. I whispered, "He's got 120 yards, and he's hitting a three wood to the wrong green."

Bondy whispered back, "Maybe he's a trick shot artist. He might be hitting a knockdown hook."

"It would be rude to interrupt him," I quipped.

Mark's ball took off like a rocket. Straight at the seventeenth. It came to rest a few feet from the cup. Alcohol, bad visibility, and athletic skill had created a hell of a shot— just at the wrong hole.

Judge Duncan ruled quickly, "Ignorance of the facts is no excuse, Mr. Harris. Did you intend to hit the ball? Did you, in fact, hit the ball there? Play it where it lies." He paused to reconsider, amending his ruling: "You lie two, but take a drop. We don't want any divots on these beautiful greens."

Bondy liked this no-nonsense judge.

A par from each team made for a half. On to eighteen.

Darkness enveloped the course. One of Bondy's new pub-supporters quietly made his way back to the pub to await the results. Thirty minutes was a very long time away from his stool.

With a series of big mounds and mean, deep bunkers running down the left side, eighteen required a long straight drive. Bondy drove right into the side of a pot bunker. He took his medicine and came out sideways. He now sat two.

Unfortunately, Mark was in the fairway after his drive, 220 yards to the pin. His favorite distance. He crushed it. Over the green. Lying two.

Taking my role as caddie seriously, I consulted the yardage book. Finding a gorse bush in it, I paced off the distance. Bondy's third shot tracked right at the pin. Unfortunately, it landed just short and rolled sheepishly down a steep embankment. Bondy gave me a quizzical look then smiled, "Sorry, partner—I thought I hit that perfectly. Might have to sack my caddie..."

Mark made a tap in putt for an easy bogey; Bondy faced a twelve-footer for the half. A few more villagers had stopped at the railing to see what was going on at 10:30 p.m. on the golf course. As they shouted their inebriated encouragement, Bondy lined up his putt. Bracing himself over the ball, Bondy hitched up his drooping pants, more in need of suspenders than a belt. Confidently, he stroked it right at the heart of the cup. It stopped just short...

He looked at the crowd and said, "Appears that I've got a Cuba...needs another revolution..."

With the ball balanced on the edge of the cup, Bondy proceeded glacially towards the hole.

Judge Duncan interceded, "Bondy, speed up that walk. I'll have no dawdling in my courtroom." Not wanting to risk contempt, Bondy tapped his ball in and offered a congratulatory handshake to his opponents.

Angus and a few other Scots led their team in a rousing rendition of "Flower of Scotland." Bondy and his diminished fan club went back to the bar to consider fighting another day.

CHAPTER XVII

~

THE BOTTLE

In the summer of 2000, we made Royal Portrush our destination. A native Northern Irishman, Grahame Jenkins, joined us. The same Grahame who had "invited" me to play Royal County Down. As Grahame matched Alan Swan in sheer output of words, there was the distinct possibility Bondy might be stuck just listening.

After meeting at the Belfast airport, Bondy, Grahame, and I jumped into our rental car for the trip to the seaside town of Portrush. With an accent and humor similar to that of David Feherty, Grahame blended in well on a Northern Irish golf trip. As Grahame told yet another story, Bondy leaned over and whispered, "Alan Swan has met his match. I sure hope these two don't start debating religion or politics."

As we neared Portrush, Grahame proudly pointed out, "The rock formation is called the Giant's Causeway. It was created as a bridge to allow our giant, Finn McCool, to fight the Scottish giant." I smiled thinking of our dueling

Irishman and Scot. Another 10,000 words from Grahame and we pulled into the Bushmills Inn Hotel, home of the world's oldest distillery, founded 1608.

Bondy looked around and remarked, "Let's see...a distillery...the smell of a peat fireplace...patrons with bar tans...and Alan Swan telling stories...just another trip to a world-ranked golf course."

Our hungry group of eight piled into a minibus headed for Darren Clarke's highly recommended restaurant.

Sitting at dinner with the three Irishmen—Grahame, Alan Swan, and Richard Webster—and Bondy was like being ringside at Ali vs. Frazier. Ali lands a punch on Frazier. Frazier swings back. Now wait—Foreman and Tyson are entering the ring! Pure mayhem. Pure listening pleasure.

"Who would be in your dream Irish foursome?"

Verbal punches thrown in all directions.

The Irish voices became indistinguishable, piling loudly on top of each other. A temporary truce as the waitress brought another round.

"Who exactly was Joe Carr?" I asked, inciting a verbal avalanche.

While the Irishmen took a sip, Bondy slipped in, "With these Irishmen, your ignorance about Joe Carr will be short-lived."

JOE CARR

As predicted they exploded in unison, "Only the greatest fecking amateur golfer since Bobby Jones." It was the last time they would speak with such precision. After that, their timing was always slightly off.

"Hold yer horses Jimmy," Bondy chimed in. "Sir Michael Bonallack tops the list as the finest amateur since Jones. But I would agree that J.B. Carr was certainly the best *Irish* amateur."

Alan Swan began, "Let me see—Joe Carr. Where should I start—"

"At the beginning of civilization. Then lead us through the life and times of Joe Carr and all of his grandchildren," Irishman Richard Webster interjected.

For Richard, the pleasure of making a 60-yard two putt—he putts from everywhere—paled to that of interrupting Alan.

As if swatting away a bothersome gnat, Alan Swan waved his hand, "Well, I would certainly be faster if I weren't interrupted every time I pause for a drink."

"An act which occurs frequently," Richard said.

Undeterred, Alan continued, "Now, let's see—Joe Carr won the British Amateur three times and played in eleven consecutive Walker Cups. I'd put those numbers up against most anybody. But the numbers are only a piece of the story. The man knew how to live and enjoy himself.

A real character, that Joe Carr. But then again, all old Irish golfers were characters."

Born in the early '20s in Dublin, Joe Carr was raised by his adopted parents, who managed the Portmarnock Golf Club. As with Laddie Lucas at Prince's, growing up at a championship golf course helped develop young Joe.

Richard then took the floor: "When asked how he managed on little more than a pound a week, Joe would reply with a wry Irish smile, 'There has never been a lack of wealthy men around who thought they could play golf.'"

A hustler, cut from the mold of Titanic Thompson.

Richard continued, "On one occasion, a penniless Joe had to make a lengthy journey to play in a golf tournament. Joe and a friend stopped by a local pool hall and played snooker until they made enough money. Not wishing to spend all of their newly obtained riches on the full train fare, they checked the clubs onto a train and rode a tandem bicycle to the event."

Alan cut back in: "I don't remember the location, but a cross-country tournament took place in the west of Ireland. It started on the first tee of one course and ended on the eighteenth green of another club. The makeshift course covered miles of pasture, graveyards, and farmland. Betting was heavy. Joe won it a few times. But one year, he barely lost because he tried to hit across a graveyard. In a God-fearing Catholic country, a graveyard was out of bounds. Two stroke penalty. Balls were expensive. He went in to retrieve it. Probably said a few Hail Marys..."

"And a few other choice fecking words," added another Irish voice.

THE BRAD AND THE BOTTLE

After a slight pause to order another round of Guinness, Alan continued, "If you're going to have a dream Irish foursome, you'd have to add The Brad."

Richard interjected, "That would be Harry Bradshaw, longtime head professional at Portmarnock. Serious golfer, that man. Won the Irish Championship ten times. The Brad and Joe Carr were referred to as the Hermitage Twins."

"Because they won the Hermitage pro-am event six times in nine years," Alan said. He wasn't ready to relinquish the floor. "Of course, the biggest story about The Brad was his near victory at The Open in 1949."

"Good feckin' story this one. Hard to imagine though," added an Irish voice.

Alan brushed off the interloper: "So, as I was saying, the year was 1949, and The Brad was playing The Open at Hoylake..."

"No. It was Sandwich..."

"You might be right about that...I'm not sure."

"So, anyway, during the second round at Sandwich, or wherever...but it was a links course. They only hold The Open on links courses—that much we know for sure. The Brad hit his drive right up the middle and, wouldn't you know, the ball rolled into a broken bottle in the fairway."

"It was in the rough," someone interjected.

"OK—maybe the rough. The Brad doesn't know what to do, and they can't find a marshal. After letting a few groups through, the Brad plays his ball as it lies, smashes the bottle, and takes a double bogey on the hole...so, as you might imagine, he's right upset—"

"He's feckin' mad."

"OK, he's fecking mad," Alan continued. "That's right. And he takes a double bogey on the next hole before he calms down. Wouldn't you know it, but he finishes the tournament in a dead tie for first place with Bobby Locke. He then, unfortunately, gets the shite kicked out of him in the playoff. The sad news is that he would have been entitled to a free drop. He should have played a provisional ball as well as the one out of the bottle."

Another Irish voice added, "Now, of course, the British newspapers reported that the bottle was a stout bottle. The Brad being an Irishman, it made for a great headline..."

"In reality, The Brad swore it was a milk bottle," Alan proclaimed.

It was now late. The bill had been paid. Three hours of banter. Only two members of the foursome were set.

The selection committee would likely reconvene at the Bushmills bar.

Another Bottle

The next day, we played Royal Portrush. Designed by Harry Colt, the course weaves between huge dunes with magnificent views of the ocean. Looking at the wild landscape separated by a few narrow fairways, Bondy proclaimed, "Is there a golf course in there?"

The high dunes formed a massive ridge, creating a sense that the course was partitioned from the rest of the world. As with so many classic courses, this would be an amazing place to go for a walk. It fit in the landscape naturally. Above all, there were several ways to get the ball in the hole and many decisions to be made on the tee box.

This natural style of golf course fell out of favor when architects made modern creations, with holes designed to show off the architect instead of the land. This unnatural style tended to present heroic shots and bunkering that demanded long, straight shots. Thinking not required. Hop in a cart and yell, "You da man."

Another Bottle

On the practice putting green, Grahame Jenkins pulled out his collection of foreign bills. A Scottish five-pound note signed by Angus after losing to Grahame at Prestwick. A $5 bill signed by Angus from Shinnecock Hills. "They're lonely, these bills. Need a fiver from a Northern Irish bank," Grahame needled.

"Customer golf," Angus replied. "Keep 'em happy or the purchase orders dry up." Finding it too delicious to refrain, Bondy added, "Speaking of customer golf, Angus, why don't you and I play our boss and our customer today in a little match? We'll probably let them win on eighteen just to make them feel good. Wouldn't want to affect bonuses or purchases orders."

Grahame hit the bid: "I think a few strokes a side should do just fine."

In the pro shop, we searched around for a suitable prize. A bottle of Bushmills Black Bush Irish Whiskey with the Royal Portrush logo caught our eyes. The assistant pro put two bottles aside for us. Bondy nodded, "That'll be a nice addition to my bar back in London."

The Match

With stakes set, the four of us teed off into an open fairway. As always, Bondy surveyed the countryside. He breathed in the fresh, salty air, then said, "Here's one for the memory banks...not often I partner with young Angus. We'll win a match...get kicked out of a retailer...get fired by our boss...and have a nice bottle of Bushmills to drown our sorrows..."

Like most links courses Portrush starts gently, the first playing slightly uphill. Three of us made par. Not Bondy. As usual, he had jumped out of the car, taken a few stiff practice swings, and butchered the first two holes.

Nobody confused Bondy for a yoga instructor.

Holes four and five were classic bite-off-all-you-can-chew doglegs guarded by fields of wind-swept, knee-high grass. On the African savanna, grass this tall would hide lions. On the windy coast of Northern Ireland, it just hid warehouse quantities of Titleist golf balls. Grahame made par. *One up.*

On the fifth green, we looked out at the island of Islay. Memories of peaty whiskies and Tex hitting it closer to the pin than Bondy that midnight flooded back. When I mentioned it on the sixth, Bondy calmly struck his shot to about five feet and said, "That one's for young Tex."

I made up and down for par. Bondy missed the birdie putt. Back in the States, Tex surely smiled.

Coming down the swooping dogleg par-five ninth hole, my caddie kept looking in the distance. I hit my drive into the deep left rough—then ripped my provisional down the middle. My caddie searched hard for my first tee shot but kept glancing past the green.

"The saddest sight in golf is watching that Union Jack get lowered as you walk down the ninth," said my caddie. We all leaned in. He continued, "That flag flies over the halfway house. When the flag is flying, the bar is open. It's a somber moment, indeed, when a slow golfer works his way up nine while we watch the flag being lowered."

Torn between the desire to find my ball and wanting to keep my caddie well oiled, I chose the latter. "How far is my second ball from the green?"

The answer came quickly from the plaintive caddie: "It's 235, sir, but into a slight breeze. Hit the same shot you hit on the last par-five. You birdied that one. Use your driver off the deck and aim left edge of the green. Should I go ahead to see where it winds up?"

His mentioning my birdie was wanton flattery.

It worked.

I temporarily forgot that I had just lost my drive in the deep rough. Handing him a twenty-pound note, I said, "Go up ahead. Get food and drinks for the group."

He moved faster than a five-year-old chasing an ice cream truck. Through enough examples, I have come to believe that giving an opponent a generous gimme frees the mind and makes way for a positive karmic boomerang.

A lot of ten-foot birdie putts go in after the putter has just said "That's good" to his opponent.

In the same karmic sense, getting my caddie a much-needed drink released all my tension. Lying three, but somehow forgetting the lost ball, I hit a driver off the deck. The ball started at the left edge of the green and faded slightly to the flag, stopping two feet from the hole. A dumbfounded Angus made a bad chip for his third shot. Then two putts. I made the putt for a par to halve the hole. Still *one up*. As we looked up, we saw the flag being lowered.

My caddie would have been late.

As we rounded the corner our caddie was sitting in front of the now closed halfway house next to a bench full of supplies. His smile was wide. But apparently his shopping list had been long on small bottles of Black Bush whiskey and short on bananas and soft drinks. Sharing a banana and a can of Coke, Angus, Bondy, Grahame, and I had a good laugh.

Renewed, my caddie gave me a line for the tenth hole. "Avoid the rough."

Coming to the fourteenth hole, Grahame and I were still *one up*. Bondy grumbled, "We'd be all square if Angus weren't giving so many shots to the North Sea Pirate, Grahame Jenkins."

There it was. The mother of all par-threes. Calamity.

The tee box stood on a hill, with a valley in front to the right and not much room left. Huge sand dunes glistened in the sun as if this were a mountain range in the morning.

Compared to this wild look, the cold, wind-whipped water in the distance looked peaceful. A mere 213 yards, this is a routine par-three—if your name happens to start with "L" and end in "OWRY."

Usually a traditionalist, Bondy surveyed the hole. "I wouldn't mind getting a stroke on this par-three. Anything on the card, Angus?"

The answer: "'Fraid not, partner."

"OK, well, here's one for the memory banks…" Bondy missed well short. And even more right. "I'm not even going after that one. Don't want to break my neck. Got enough memories of Calamity. Anyway, Angus will cover me."

He did. Fifteen feet from the pin. Barely missed the putt.

Grahame and I each made up and down from Locke's hollow short of the green. Still *one up.*

"It's unfortunate that putt missed. Good roll, though," Grahame remarked, "You sure don't see many natural birdies on Calamity. But you should clear that missed historic opportunity from your mind right away."

Angus hit his next tee shot in the deep rough. Bondy covered him.

On sixteen I three-putted. *All square.*

The par-five seventeen featured a massive bunker, guarding the right side of the fairway. Three of us hit our drives there. Grahame and I had to come out backwards. Our miracle shots didn't work. *One down.*

On the long par-four eighteenth, I got a stroke. Angus and I both reached the green in two, about twenty feet from the hole. Angus was away. I was lying net one.

Then things changed.

Angus drained his putt. Birdie.

"We were the Americans at Brookline after Leonard made his putt...no players' wives jumping up and down," Bondy retold later in the bar. "Just a few disheveled caddies with small whiskey bottles falling out of their pockets."

Instead of two-putt par, I *had* to make birdie to win the hole and halve the match. I lined up my twenty-footer. Struck it exactly how I wanted. It tracked straight at the cup...then shaved the edge for a meaningless tap in par.

Match over. One down.

Angus and Bondy skipped to the pro shop to collect their bottles.

Back in London, Bondy stored his on his mantel. He frequently sent us photos.

Enid Day

CHAPTER XVIII

~

THE LAST HOLE

In 2005, eleven years after we met, Bondy announced his plans to retire. I had known the moment would come. It still hit me hard. Bondy was one of those people who never really leaves a company—he was an institution.

The last day had arrived. Mark Harris, Goetz, and I arranged to play one final round with an employed Bondy. Bondy chose Glasgow Gailes—where it all began. The course was a short wedge from the factory. He caddied there as a kid. Was hired to repair clubs next door. Became the managing director.

Bondy made a mark on all he touched. He was a tough task master with a huge heart. We both came from similar working-class towns. A disciplined culture—Army and Merchant Navy—molded each of us in our teens. We appreciated hard work. We loved to sell. We loved to be in charge. We loved to win.

To me, Bondy represented far more than just an excellent businessman with a true sense of obligation and decency. He was my golf mentor. He was my adversary. He was my partner. He was my true friend. In his words, "We've sure gotten some things done, young Mr. Reese. Great times in the office...and we managed to play a few golf matches."

We had made innumerable deposits into the memory banks.

We hungered for more.

Pulling into the driveway at Glasgow Gailes, I looked over my shoulder at the neighboring course. My mind drifted to us huddling in a snow-covered bunker. I smiled. It seemed like just yesterday.

The weather on this day was calm, with intermittent splashes of sun coming through the puffy clouds. No rain. No howling wind. The grass swayed ever so slightly in the breeze. Almost as if nature decided to take a break to watch Bondy retire.

Goetz, Mark, and I changed into golf clothes then ate a few sandwiches before heading to the putting green to meet Bondy. Then the call came: "I'm stuck at work. I'll be joining you for a drink after the round." Bondy was delayed at the office. I tried not to display my disappointment, mustering a fake, light-hearted smile.

I fooled no one.

Four holes into our round, Mark and Goetz burst into huge grins as I prepared to hit my second shot. Coming towards us with his sticks, a beaming Bondy called out, "I skipped out of work. They're not going to fire me. I'd hate to miss the chance to take a few pounds from young Mr. Reese. Might need it for my retirement."

Let's go.

We agreed to play a thirteen-hole match. Ten pounds. Not a lot, but a token. In a twist that had taken a few years, Bondy no longer gave me strokes. I now gave him more than a few. He gladly took them. I was now a five, and he was playing to a twelve. It took a bit of time to sort out shots on the thirteen remaining holes. We got it straight...after some haggling.

Both of us really wanted this round together. I had left the company three years before. Bondy's retirement represented a cutting of ties with the past. The proximity to our factory made the match that much more poignant.

In the beginning, I had been inspired by Angus and intimidated by Bondy. Then still inspired by Angus and amused by Bondy. Now, I just felt fondness for both.

Don't mistake fondness for complacency. I still wanted to beat the hell out of him. He felt the same.

Ever the Scot, he pulled a slightly scuffed-up ball out of his bag and rooted around for a tee and a ball marker. Then, putting the tee in the ground, he smiled and

197

said, "Here's one for the memory banks...likely going to have to hire an investment advisor to handle the money I'll be taking from young Mr. Reese today." With that opening, he swatted a low runner down the middle. It ran like a scalded dog on the burned-out fairway.

Let the match begin.

Giving him strokes still seemed odd. He liked it. As he had done to me repeatedly over the years, I frequently reminded him he was running out of strokes. Soon we would be playing even up. He just smiled.

Coming up to the eighteenth, with the match *all square,* an employed Bondy and I braced for one last dual. The emotion was simply too great for me. I made a fast backswing and blocked my drive into the hay on the right. I needed a gap wedge to advance the ball.

I watched helplessly as Bondy pulled out his trademark five wood, the head of which was no bigger than a one-pound coin. I had been the victim of this club so many times. It was the personification of Bondy's will. He gave it

Enid Day

a lash. Low burning trajectory directly at the pin.

Thrilled, he held his pose. He had me. He knew it. He looked over at me and smiled.

The ball hit the center of the green and rocketed forward. Kept rolling. Finally coming to rest about twenty yards past the green in a small clump of uneven grass. I offered some advice: "On links courses, you might want to hit the ball in front of the green and let it run up."

"I taught you how to play this game. I am now going to show you how to make a wee up and down for a one up victory," he laughed. "It'll be a good one for this old Scot to win."

I choked down on my nine iron, put the ball back in my stance, and hit my 100-yard shot with a low trajectory. It landed well in front of the green, chasing up ten feet from the pin. Bondy shook his head. "Still some work to do for your par. Have I mentioned you skimming the edge on eighteen at Royal Portrush?"

Yes.

Several times.

Bondy had a tough lie that prevented him from getting a clean club face on the ball. Still, he chipped to about fifteen feet. As I had seen him do so many times before, Bondy crouched over his putter with total concentration. He hitched up his slightly baggy pants and eyed the hole. He wanted this one badly. It came off the club with a nice roll. The line looked good—straight towards the cup.

Then, at the last second, it veered away. It settled an inch past the hole.

No sound. Just me, smiling.

Now it was my turn. The vaults of my memory banks opened. Missed putts against Bondy on Lundin Links. Western Gailes. Littlestone. Royal Cinque et Trois. Prince's. And Royal Portrush. I thought of the cuff links that read "real world, no gimmes" he and Angus had given me.

But years of playing with the formerly intimidating Bondy had strengthened me. He no longer tap-danced inside my head.

My mind went blank. All was silent. The cup grew.

I took a firm stance and brought the putter head back. I accelerated as the Scotty Cameron came forward. The ball left the club face with that beautiful topspin roll that creates an energy of its own.

Nothing could stop it. Nothing did.

It made a much better sound than Bondy smiling.

In one motion, I took off my hat and reached out with my hand.

"Welcome to retirement, Mr. Bond."

Years later, one of the Irishmen asked Bondy what it was like to work at Wilson.

He said, "I worked there 41 years. I skipped out on my last day to play a match against Luke Reese...lost ten pounds on the last hole. I don't remember much else."

Chapter XIX

~

Final Memories

After our round, Bondy and his beloved wife Margaret moved resolutely and contentedly into retirement. Instead of rallying his sales team, he now entertained his two kids and grandchildren.

We often met in Dublin, for a few rounds at Portmarnock. As we teed off, he would stick his tee in the ground and say, "Of course, young Angus won't be joining us. He's scared of this place." Then he'd hit 220 down the middle with a little left to right tail, and we would be off. Just another one for the memory banks.

On my 55th birthday at Portmarnock, master-of-ceremonies Bondy started play with a 200-yard drive down the middle. Now solidly in his 70s, Bondy played to a fifteen. His swing was no longer powerful. But beware, he still knew how to get the ball in the hole.

Finishing the morning round, we all showered and donned blazers for lunch. Bondy declined the second round. Thirty-six was no longer in the cards. I offered to get a caddie, but he responded, "Mr. Reese, you're no longer young Mr. Reese...but you're not yet old Mr. Reese... one day you'll understand. This old back needs a comfortable chair and a wee dram...with a nice view of you struggling on a windy links course. I'll be ready to take you on tomorrow."

The next day, I videoed Bondy taking his swing on the first tee. He hit a low runner right down the middle. What else. It was accompanied by a clamor of Irish voices. "Good shot." "Well struck." "What a beauty."

At dinner we drank an excellent Rioja with steaks in the clubhouse at Portmarnock. Life was great. That night we slept like bears in hibernation. The next morning, we played The European Club, known for its holes along the coast, with railroad sleepers supporting the bunkers.

Unfortunately, the birthday trip had to end.

As we split at the Dublin Airport, Bondy pulled me aside. "I'm not sure I've ever truly thanked you...you gave me a chance...and I did a halfway decent job." He smiled.

"Bondy, I called your number. You scored the goals." The lump in my throat rose. "And you made me a halfway decent golfer."

"It's all come together...still might make you putt the occasional three-footer...you play the game the way it was meant to be played," Bondy answered. "I almost turned one American golfer into a Scot. Maybe I should open a match play training academy."

In a rare moment, we hugged. I cried all the way to the check-in counter.

Having learned from Bondy, I passed on his lessons to new golfers. They play fast match play. They celebrate the rub of the green. They compete on every hole. They love the courses on which this amazing game is played. They don't let their bad golf ruin the good time of others.

Several do not know Bondy. But they have felt his influence. My favorite playing partner recently said, "It's raining...we'll have the course to ourselves." That golfer can frequently be found next to a fireplace with coffee and a golf architecture book.

Bondy cancelled the next two golf trips. For our trip to Dornoch in 2017, he called, saying, "Afraid I have to miss this one. No golf due to back problems. I'll get it all sorted by next year. Dornoch...wonderful course. What a comeback we had against Angus and his merry band of buccaneers. Still need to check those handicaps."

"Would a stroke a hole get you up there?"

That got a small chuckle.

Despite the banter, I knew something was wrong. He would only miss a trip for family graduations, weddings, or other major life events.

Even with a bad back Bondy would have entertained us. We loved hearing his stories. He loved telling them. Bondy was like a jukebox. Enter a course name or date, wait for the memory to queue, then sit back and listen. "Speaking of Royal Troon, have I mentioned what Sam Snead told me once...now Sam was in his late 80s at the time and he was standing next to Patty Berg...it wasn't the most delicate comment I ever heard...might have shocked old Patty..."

One Sunday morning in the spring of 2019, Angus called.

"Luker, it's Gus. Bondy's not doing well..."

I called Bondy immediately. "Sorry, Mr. Reese, I'm not able to play much for a bit...the doctors don't know what it is...but I can't walk more than a hole...my legs just aren't working.

"Afraid you'll have to settle with me having beaten you almost every time we played. Glad I caught you early!"

I barely managed a response.

A month later, he called me.

Motor Neuron Disease.

Amyotrophic Lateral Sclerosis (ALS).

Lou Gehrig's Disease.

The room blurred.

To raise Bondy's spirits, we set up a Masters pool among Angus, Bondy, Neil Parker—the one who played the piano too loudly and incurred Tony Hercus' wrath at the Marine Highland Hotel in Troon—and I. Bondy picked first. Maximum banter. They took all the good healthy players. They stuck me with a long shot named Tiger. Bondy provided email updates every few holes. I rolled my fictional winnings into the next Major.

For the US Open, we had a group call after two rounds. "Tournament looks great...never quite made it to Pebble. Never got to Luffness New either."

"You made it to a few tracks, Bondy," Angus added. "Plenty of Doak points."

In late June, Angus arranged for a few of us to surprise Bondy with a visit. The affection burning in his eyes struck me to the core. I had to leave the room frequently to wipe away tears. He called Margaret and Angus into the room: "Could you see if anything in the dining room might interest young Mr. Reese?"

Angus returned with the unopened bottle of Bushmills whiskey with a Royal Portrush logo that I'd signed almost twenty years before. Bondy could no longer hold it. Angus stood next to him and cradled it in his hands as Bondy recounted multiple stories that had been so dear to us.

He talked of not existing at Luffness New, "You are a never, never." Then he told us about Rub of the Green. The snow at Western Gailes.

"So, Angus, my five wood on eighteen inspired Pádraig to win three Majors."

He then repeated the words "Royal Cinque et Trois" a few times just to make sure we remembered. He talked of the UK reps calling the bartender a miserable wanker.

The memory banks overflowed.

A few weeks later, I got the call from Margaret.

"Your friend Bondy is in a better place. As he was leaving, he could no longer speak. But he typed a message to you, *"Tell Luke...thank you for having faith in me...I enjoyed beating him on the golf course."*

Over our collective tears, I am not sure whether she said *"being with"* or *"beating."* Even if Margaret said the former, Bondy meant the latter.

His Bushmills whiskey bottle, five wood, and putter are now lovingly displayed in Scotland, back home.

Brendan Savage

A Note from Neil Parker

～

I was fortunate enough to share not just one, but two different passions with Bondy. Of course, we were both fanatical golfers, enjoying many matches together on some of the UK's finest courses, including his beloved home club, Cuddington. Our second shared interest was less common but even more magical. The piano. Those 88 black and white keys held a lifelong fascination for both of us. As much as we loved striding lush fairways side by side, nothing quite matched the unbridled joy we got from countless occasions leading raucous singalongs in hotel bars around Europe during the fifteen years we worked together. We were very good for bar takings, but neither of us could recall once being offered a cut. I'll never forget his favourite song. It's impossible to forget because he made me play it every time we found ourselves together at the ivories. And there couldn't be a more appropriate tune for a guy so passionate about golf and piano. I see his smiling face every time I play "The Green, Green Grass of Home."

A Note from Ken Macpherson

~

At first Allan enjoyed just the playing of the game, but soon it was the history, the equipment used, the courses, and especially the life and times of all of the great players throughout the ages that interested him.

Allan's connections in golf gave him the opportunity to play on many of the great courses, yet when he came to talk about his experiences it seemed that those with whom he was playing were more important than the venue or how he had played. Anyone who thinks that golf is a selfish game never played golf with Allan Bond.

When on his game, Allan could play to a low handicap, and just to be in his company on the course was a joy. "Och Allan!" was as bad as the language ever got. To Allan, winning was good, and losing was an awful lot better than not playing at all.

Modesty, honesty, integrity, and loyalty. Allan had the lot.

A Note from Angus Moir

～

It's been over a year, and I still can't believe he's gone. He was a West Coast Scot; I was an East Coaster. But somehow, we made do. I will always recall his passion for life and how much I learned from him—on and off the course. Over the 30+ years we knew each other, we golfed, we sang, we debated, we laughed, and we, for sure, sampled the odd whisky. One of my fondest memories will be of Bondy, a few whiskys in, sitting by the piano or listening to some old crooner. He loved music. His favorite thing to scat when he sang was "itchiecoo." None of us quite knew what it meant, but there was no doubt in our minds that he was having a blast. Whenever I step on a course, I can't help but think of his golf game. He had a bit of Arnie to him. I think that's how he'd like me to remember him. Itchiecoo, Bondy!

ACKNOWLEDGMENTS

~

To Margaret Bond—

English teacher and beloved wife to Bondy. You gave me great historical background and fixed many of my grammatical mistakes. You filled me with joy when you said, "Ken Macpherson and I could hear Bondy's voice." Above all, you paid me the highest compliment by saying I had captured the essence of our dear friend and your soulmate.

To Mom—

Any typos in this book are my responsibilty. They got there after you finished proofreading. You provided me with endless love and support, and your grammar lessons have never been forgotten...although they've been occasionally ignored.

To Enid Day—

Thank you for your breathtaking illustrations. You helped bring the story to life. Your paintings will hang in Scotland next to Bondy's five wood.

To Maddie—

Having one of my daughters edit this story and make it dramatically better has been an incredible gift. The back and forth on each chapter has been time I would never trade. You transformed this book. You cut out the boring parts and accentuated the essence of the story. You preserved and honored my voice. You launched social media. You built the web site. You researched, developed, and implemented our marketing strategy. You designed the cover. You laid out the book. You negotiated on behalf of the caddies. You managed the workstreams, making sure we got the revised drafts and artwork done. You exceeded my sky-high expectations. Tuition payments were well spent. This could not have been more fun.

To Olivia—

You want to heal the world. You bring your strength and confidence to everything you do. You are wickedly intelligent, hardworking, kind, and hilarious. And most importantly, you have such a steadfast sense of self. You inspire me every day.

To Brian Lewis—

Wow. You grabbed this and attacked. You met and exceeded timeframes. You responded with cheer and passion. You made us reach higher. You made me think

I was funny. Having a publisher operate on a Luke and Maddie time frame amazed us. One of us got up early. The other one stayed up late. Projects and tasks came at all hours. Thank you for agreeing to read the first chapter. Thank you even more for calling back in ten minutes and saying, "You can write."

I would like to express my most sincere thanks to those who helped read multiple chapters and drafts, found and arranged photos, and reconstructed dialogue during this COVID-19 isolation. You all gave incredible advice and had to suffer with my "let's get this done now" personality.

Jason Adel	Mark Harris
Margaret Bond	Everett Heckman
Alistair Brown	George Hodges
John Connolly	Francis Howley
Frank Clay	Martyn Huish
Steve Clifford	Kari Kauniskangas
Jack Davis	Mark Lampert
Sean Fay	Goetz Laue
Tom Gilbert	Brian Lewis
Pat Gunning	John MacCarthy
Lucas Hall	Ian Mackenzie
Mike Hall	Richard Mackenzie-Smith
Neil Hampton	Ken Macpherson

Todd Martin

Sara Mess

Scott Mahoney

Angus Moir

Jaime Morales

Ran Morrissett

Chris Murray

Angela Negrete

Dave O'Connell

Neil Parker

Will Plunkett

John Preschlack

Greg Purcell

David Reese

Gil Reese

Lou Reese

Martha Grace Reese

Paul Reid

Wes Roberts

Jeff Sernick

Eric Schultz

Bradley Smith

Alan Swan

David Thomson

John Wallace

Michael Wallace

Sarah Wallace

Ken Weyand

I hope we can manage to steal an extra eighteen holes from life together soon.

Chelsea Sorbo

ABOUT THE AUTHOR

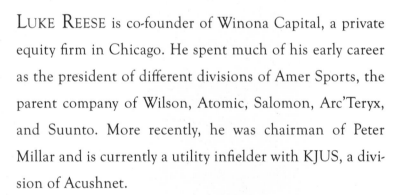

LUKE REESE is co-founder of Winona Capital, a private equity firm in Chicago. He spent much of his early career as the president of different divisions of Amer Sports, the parent company of Wilson, Atomic, Salomon, Arc'Teryx, and Suunto. More recently, he was chairman of Peter Millar and is currently a utility infielder with KJUS, a division of Acushnet.

After serving in the United States Army in military intelligence, he graduated from DePauw University and the University of Michigan Law School. He later worked as an attorney at Latham & Watkins.

He lives in Colorado and spends as much time as possible in Great Britain and Ireland. He has two amazing daughters, Olivia and Madeline.

Frank Clay

ABOUT THE EDITOR

MADELINE REESE was the 2016 Thomas B. Wanamaker English Language Prize winner at Princeton University. After four years at Credit Suisse, she is pursuing her MBA at Northwestern University – Kellogg School of Management. She loves to sing and act and is learning to play fast golf.